CHARISMATIC SUPERSTITIONS
& MISCONCEPTIONS

JIM CROFT

E**v**ergreen
PRESS

Charismatic Superstitions And Misconceptions
by Jim Croft
Copyright ©2001 Jim Croft
All rights reserved. This book is protected under the copyright laws of the United States of America. This book may not be copied or reprinted for commercial gain or profit. The use of short quotations or occasional page copying for personal or group study is permitted and encouraged. Permission will be granted upon request. Unless otherwise identified, Scripture quotations are from the New King James Version of the Bible.

ISBN 1-58169-058-4
For Worldwide Distribution
Printed in the U.S.A.

Evergreen Press
P.O. Box 91011 • Mobile, AL 36691
800-367-8203
E-mail: EvergreenBooks@aol.com

TABLE OF CONTENTS

ACKNOWLEDGMENT

I would like to thank Eileen Hubers for her tireless work in helping me prepare the original manuscript for the publisher.

DEDICATION

This book is dedicated to the members
of Good News Church and Gold Coast Christian Church
whom I have served over the past 25 years.
Their faithful indulgence and gracious encouragement
as I have expounded the views found in these chapters
is greatly appreciated.

INTRODUCTION

For a number of years I have been meditating on what I consider to be a perplexing enigma. Many believers have the impression that the primary way that they can please God is to fill their lives with as many overtly religious activities as possible. Some describe the ideal vocational environment as one where they would have unrestrained liberty to punctuate every conversation with Christian jargon. During church services, they glow with the vibrant confidence that they have heavenly approval. It is as though they believe that they are fulfilling the zenith of life's purpose solely when they are singing hymns, testifying, and listening to sermons. The enigma is that when life's necessities call them to be occupied with other equally legitimate pursuits, the quality of the confident glow that they have heavenly approbation seems to mysteriously wane.

The reality of this can be discerned through the level of dissatisfaction that many Christians express about their marriages, vocations, and their lives in general. Alarming statistics bear evidence of this. There is no significant difference in the divorce rate, frequency of vocational change, or use of anti-depressants among professing believers and unbelievers. The presence of this enigma and its tragic consequences has gradually caused me to come to a disconcerting suspicion. I suspect that it is probable that there is something amiss in the spiritual diet of Christians that blurs their worldview. This toxic element reduces the arenas of life in which Christians have liberty to experience the abundance of life that Christ promised.

I have been relieved by my discussions with other Christian leaders to learn that I am not alone in my suspicions.

More than a few have indicated that they are coming to the same conclusion. Some concur that the phenomena could compare with the effects of radioactive fall-out on the fields in which livestock graze and on the food crops that are eventually sold in our grocery stores. The atmosphere of our churches and (what we thought was) the sincere milk of the Word we were feeding to the faithful are actually tainted with unholy "spiritual radiation." It is producing a hybrid mutation of Christianity that is inconsistent with the biblical presentation of authentic Christian life. This contamination is, in part, the fall-out from teaching that explosively emphasizes a division between the secular and the spiritual. Biblically there is no such division because all aspects of life are described as spiritual, even though they are not all primarily religious. God's divine influence and pleasure can be experienced in every arena of life, though every arena may not be overtly religious in its content and exercise.

This line of reasoning might be clarified by considering two things: 1) how and why God created man; and, 2) the life of Jesus. As we do this it is important to keep in mind that every Christian should be able to enjoy their relationship with the Lord, but it is even more essential that we become the type of people whom God Himself enjoys. We were created in God's image and for His pleasure (Gen. 1:26-27; Rev. 4:11 KJV). The fact that we are created in His image indicates that all of our talents, interests, and our abilities to find fulfillment in creative endeavors are reflections of His nature. After He created man, He placed him in a garden for creative productivity rather than a church building for the observance of religious practices (Gen. 2:15). Apparently God derives great pleasure from watching us enjoy non-religious activities. This is clear because He designed life in such a manner that the mundane, by necessity, occupies the major portion of our time.

He could have easily required that we set aside six days per week as Sabbaths for worship and one day for routine duties if He actually put a premium on worship above work. He enjoys watching a mother diapering her infant and a father laboring to provide for his family as much as He does when each is engaged in worship or witnessing. The film "Chariots of Fire" featured a Scottish missionary who was challenged by his mission board to refrain from running in marathons. Their concern was that it was not a worthy use of his energies. His response reveals much about the breadth of God's interests. He said, "I feel the pleasure of God when I am running."

We reflect the nature of God by the type of people with whom we choose to fellowship. Normally we seek the companionship of those that are secure in who they are and express enthusiasm for their vocations and the projects of others. Conversely, we tend to avoid people who are insecure about their relationship with us. Most of us find it unpleasant to be friends with those who are frustrated with their lives. Unquestionably, God loves those who are insecure, frustrated, and needy. So should we. He graciously meets their needs and visits them with episodes of His comforting presence. So should we. It is possible, however, that like us, He finds pleasure in and prefers to abide with those who enjoy life in general.

This is borne out in the life of Jesus. It was a joy for the heavenly Father to observe His Son growing up and developing into a master carpenter during the 30 years before He launched into "full-time" ministry. God the Father gave testimony of this at Jesus' water baptism when He spoke from heaven and said, "You are my beloved Son, in You I am well pleased" (Luke 3:22). Up until this event, Jesus had not preached a single sermon or healed anyone. His life was that of an ordinary man of His day. He worked long hours to earn a living; He had relatives and close personal friends with whom He chose to fellowship. Like most Jews, He observed the Sabbath and the various religious holidays. It is evident that He looked forward to His public ministry. Nonetheless, no one could imagine that He moped in agonized frustration until the day He was released to minister. To the contrary, He said that He knew that He always did the things that pleased His Father (Jn. 8:29). The word *always* is all-inclusive. This indicates that He understood that God enjoyed Him when He swept the floor of the carpenter shop as much as He did when He later raised the dead. Unlike many sincere, contemporary Christians, there is no evidence that He so longed for religious pursuits that He felt miserably unfulfilled when He was occupied with the ordinary activities of life.

It is my conviction that teachings that condition people to sense fulfillment only when they're engaged in religious pursuits and not in other daily occupations are counterproductive to the propagation of the Gospel. Such doctrines cause people to plummet into that which 1 Peter 1:18 (NIV) calls "... the empty way of life handed down to you from your forefathers." The quality of their lives spirals into emptiness because they have been robbed of the capacity to enjoy the pleasures that are divinely designed to comprise life here on earth. They have difficulty in enjoying their vocations, avocations, families, and acquaintances that might not share their views. The tragic end result is twofold. They cannot truly experience the Lord in His fullness, and God misses the opportunity to enjoy them to the optimum extent. In addition, they present a skewed picture to the unsaved of what the Christian life is all about. The unconverted may be spiritually uninformed, but they are not undiscerning. They comprehend as much from the quality of our lives as they do from the testimonies we offer. They are attracted to us when we exhibit wholeness and a zest for life. If we demonstrate an existence that appears complicated rather than enhanced by our faith, they perceive it as unattractive and uninviting.

This book is offered to help uncomplicate Christians' lives by examining some of the doctrines and practices that have elements of toxicity. Hopefully it will also enable believers to find relaxed joy in all aspects of life and increase the potential for greater numbers of the unsaved to interpret us as refreshing and intriguing people.

Chapter 1

Formulas Not Based on Faith

During the Jesus movement I often ministered deliverance to the hippies who were being converted in our city. On one occasion a young woman was having an unusually violent struggle to find relief. Suddenly, as she thrashed about, a demonic spirit repeatedly spoke out from her vocal cords, "It's her cross that keeps me in." I reacted by insisting that she take the beaded necklace and wooden cross from her neck. She was gloriously set free. Her demeanor was totally transformed as she joyfully wept and praised the Lord for her freedom. Ironically, although she was immediately liberated, it was months before I realized that I had slipped into a form of religious bondage.

My success with the young woman caused me to believe that all forms of religious art attracted evil spirits. I ritualized its removal and destruction whenever I performed an exorcism. The second commandment was my proof text: "You shall not make for yourself a carved image, or any likeness of anything that is in heaven above, or that is in the earth beneath..." Though many people were set free, there were several respected Christians who voiced concerns that my posture was excessive. This compelled me to examine the Scriptures. To my chagrin, I found that gifted artisans had been filled with the Spirit to mold images of living things (Ex. 35:30-35). The fixtures of the tabernacle of Moses and Solomon's temple were indeed decorated with cherubs, oxen, lions, and flowers (Ex. 25:33; 1 Kings 7:28-29). And so I repented of my naive adherence to a form of deception, which I now term as a "charismatic superstition." I use the word *superstition* because of its connotation that adherence to or neglect of certain beliefs or rituals of ministry will bring either blessed or negative consequences. Charismatic superstitions are aberrations of faith that have evolved from misconceptions about what the Bible teaches in relation to apprehending God's favor and ministering His redemptive mercies.

This book addresses 79 charismatic superstitions and misconceptions that are currently being propagated and embraced in the Church. They are based on partial truths and/or exaggerations of biblical truths that are energized by subjective revelations and seemingly validating experiences. The manner in which these aberrations of faith emerge is very subtle. They are spawned from our legitimate zeal to serve the Lord and bless others through what we have heard and experienced.

It works something like this: We hear or develop a teaching that is a mixture of mostly truth and some deception. We activate it in our lives or ministry to others and experience positive results. We naively presume that it was our belief or methodology rather than the mercy of God that brought the subsequent blessings. We fail to discern that God is lovingly benevolent and will use even imperfect means to grant us His mercies. We mistakenly believe that experiences of His blessings inevitably indicate that He endorses our beliefs and methods. Then our legalistic tendencies break forth, and we begin to dogmatically assert our misconceptions and superstitions as vital truths.

However, God wants us all to understand that even though His mercy motivates Him to bless less than ideal methods, He has not exempted us from cultivating a love for the truth. He expects us to look past our experiences and to reflect on the cumulative counsel of the Word of God in our search for truth (2 Thes. 2:10-11). If we fail to do so, we risk embracing delusions that can undermine our credibility in the Christian community and among unbelievers. Then if we become isolated from the objective light of fellowship with other Christians, it becomes easier for us to be further entangled by views that are departures from the eternal truths of God's Word (1 Jn. 1:7).

Legalism is the primary culprit that motivates us to perpetuate these aberrations of truth. There is something within our fallen nature that drives us to attempt to reduce the paths to God's blessings to rigid formulas. Legalism is the cruel two-edged sword of hyper-religiosity. With one edge, it cuts into the souls of Christians who come to live in fear of breaking a taboo of their group. Those deemed faithful tend to relate to God and to one another mainly on the basis of an agreement about what *should be forbidden* (focusing on the negative), as opposed to what they *can do* through Christ and the encouragement of their church (focusing on the positive).

The other edge of the sword discourages the unconverted from looking to Christianity as a viable source of comfort and joy. Many of these unbelievers are sensible, productive people who are cautious about visiting Christian services simply because those who invite them have espoused beliefs and rituals that seem complicated and rigid. Other unbelievers have been loaded with condemnation by the world for their ineptness and so are timid about exposing themselves to religious institutions that focus on openly criticizing those (both within and without) who do not meet their standards. Many sinners would welcome an invitation to have a loving Lord come into their lives and reshape their values. However, they are not attracted by the prospect of having to jump through our spiritual hoops in order to be accepted.

Biblical Christianity is not a religion that puts a priority on rules and regulations. It is a religion that emphasizes harmonious relationships with our fellow man through our submission to the lordship of Jesus. Within the faith, there are few absolutes and many variables in relation to how our faith is to be expressed. Love, faith, knowing the voice of God, regular fellowship, and marital fidelity are *absolutes*. *When* one prays, *how* one is baptized, *what* one prefers to eat and drink, *which* amoral pleasures one can choose to enjoy, and *the steps* to entering greater depths of God's freedom are *variables*. A disappointment of contemporary Christianity is that each group *majors* on their restrictions in the variables and *minors* on the power of the absolutes. It could be that the Lord might withhold a great harvest until these issues are resolved. It would be tragic to have millions express the desire to enter God's kingdom and subsequently be driven away by our superstitious legalisms.

The following chapters provide examples of the superstitions and misconceptions that are currently being circulated among Spirit-filled Christians. Each superstition and misconception will be identified as such and is numbered within its respective chapter. Each one will be followed by Scripture-based logic that might prompt some to reevaluate their positions. To fully understand the content of each point, it is necessary that the accompanying Scripture references also be read. The final chapter contains a doctrinal foundation that hopefully will prove helpful in deterring the emergence and acceptance of these aberrations of faith.

Chapter 2

The Godhead

My counseling sessions with troubled saints from diverse denominations has helped me to see that a better understanding of some of the basic characteristics of God Himself can minister peace to their souls. For example, many are insecure about their ability to please God. I have found that this concern is often relieved as I share that the same Father, Son, and Holy Spirit who together as One Godhead declared, "Let us make man in our image," also declared that they were individually chosen for adoption into the family of God.

I try to convey to these people that at some point in eternity past, all of us were fully seen, known, and personally discussed by name within the council of the Godhead. Their unified wisdom and good pleasure dictated that we would be an excellent choice to be accepted in the Beloved as a holy and blameless child of His love (Eph. 1:4-8). God knows the end from the beginning. There is nothing in our character that has ever mystified or shocked Him. Playwrights write a play and then select the cast. God selected the cast for each generation and then wrote the script. It is not our lot to be a hapless victim of any supposed rough seas of divine whim. We were chosen and uniquely gifted to represent God to this generation (2 Tim. 1:9). He unashamedly delights in us.

The following are some common *misconceptions about God in bold print*, followed by biblically based statements that bring His light and clarity to each point:

1) **Misconception: There is no such thing as the Trinity because the Bible says that there is one God and that God is one.**

The members of the Godhead are called the Trinity because they are one in their unity. As three uniquely distinct Persons, they flow in perfectly harmonious agreement. Though most Christians believe in the Trinity, they find the concept perplexing. The mystery centers around the Scriptures which say that there is one God, and that God is One (Deut. 6:4).

It is confusing because it is our tendency to think numerically when we hear the word "one." In the Scriptures, "one" is often used to describe unity between separate individuals. Husband and wife are called one, yet they are distinctively different individuals in their sex and function (Eph. 5:31). First Corinthians 6:17 relates that those who are joined to Jesus in the faith are one with Him in spirit. First Corinthians 7:1 says that we are to cleanse ourselves of all filthiness of spirit. If the aforementioned oneness in spirit indicated a numerical value— becoming truly one—it would imply the unthinkable. It is impossible for Jesus to have filthiness in His Spirit. We can only conclude that the phrase "one spirit with Him" refers to *unity* rather than *number.*

There are many incidents in the Bible where members of the Godhead are portrayed as functioning simultaneously in the same location. In the book of Daniel, the divine Son of Man was seen receiving an everlasting kingdom from God the

Father, the Ancient of Days (Dan. 7:13-14). When the prophet John baptized Christ, he heard the Father speaking from heaven, and he saw the Holy Spirit coming upon Jesus like a dove (Matt. 3:16-17). If God the Father, God the Son, and God the Holy Spirit were actually a singular divine person, it would indicate that Jesus was performing simultaneously as a ventriloquist and an illusionist.

In the beginning when God created Adam, He discussed the prospect with His pre-incarnate eternal Son and the person of the Holy Spirit. As we have seen in the beginning of this chapter, He said, "Let us make man in our image" (Gen. 1:26). Another time, we can see that He was not speaking to Himself when David recalled that "The Lord said to my Lord, 'Sit at My right hand, till I make your enemies your footstool'" (Psa. 110:1). In that instance, God the Father was speaking to His divine Son.

2) **Misconception: Jesus was poor.**

While Jesus was on this earth, He walked in faith for God's blessings vocationally, both as a carpenter and as the founder of a very successful ministry. Before going into "full-time ministry," He was well known as the son of Joseph, the carpenter of Nazareth (Matt. 13:55). The implication is that Joseph was a fairly successful, well-known carpenter. While working in the secular field, Jesus completely fulfilled the Old Testament law (Matt. 5:17). He had to observe all of the various Sabbaths contained in Judaism, meaning that He took over 70 days off from any labor whatsoever each year. It was also mandatory for Him to make three yearly pilgrimages from Nazareth to Jerusalem for Passover, Pentecost, and the Feast of Tabernacles. He could not have afforded to take the time off unless He had a lucrative business.

Contrary to religious tradition, Jesus was not a poor, itinerant prophet who traveled about from place to place with a team of beggarly disciples who never knew where their next meal was coming from. Jesus had a treasurer, named Judas, who stole money from the offering box (John 12:6). Yet Jesus still had sufficient funds to give to the poor and pay the salaries and travel expenses of His team of 12 men. Most of the apostles had families at home while they traveled with Jesus for three and a half years. It is unreasonable to think that they left their families penniless while they spent their days with the loving King of Kings. Furthermore, Jesus was regularly entertained and supported by wealthy people (Luke 8:2-3). Most of our well-known healing evangelists do very well financially. It is naive to presume that people did not give very generously to the flawless ministry of Jesus Christ. The sinful woman who broke the alabaster vase of costly perfume to anoint His head and feet had paid the equivalent of a year's wages for it (John 12:5 NIV). In our currency that would be around $22,000. Most everyone would agree that any minister who could send His disciple to retrieve a gold coin from a fish's mouth to pay taxes could not possibly qualify to be called poor. And finally, His robe was seamless and so expensive that the Roman soldiers who crucified Him would not tear it in order to divide it among themselves, so they gambled for it.

3) Misconception: The Holy Spirit is not a distinct member of the Godhead. "It" is a spiritual force that mystically emanates from the presence of God to effect His benevolent desires for mankind.

The Scriptures never refer to the Holy Spirit by the impersonal word "it." The Holy Spirit is referred to by the personal pronoun "He" or by personal names that describe His functions. Some of these names are: the Comforter, the Helper, the Spirit of truth, and the Spirit of the Lord (John 14:16-19,26; 2 Cor. 3:17-18). The three of them—the Father, the Son, and the Holy

Spirit—are depicted as three distinct divine members of the Godhead who are co-eternal in their existence, co-equal in their divinity, and co-essential in their diverse functions. The Apostle Peter clearly understood that the Holy Spirit is God. When he rebuked Ananias for his duplicity, he inquired of him, "Why has Satan filled your heart to lie to the Holy Spirit....You have not lied to men but to God" (Acts 5:3-4).

Psychologists agree that there are three elements which are needed to qualify one as a person: will, knowledge, and emotion. The Holy Spirit has all three. His *will* is exemplified in that He has the ability to express His opinions (Acts 13:2, 15:28). He goes where He wills and does whatever He desires for whomever He wishes (John 3:8; 1 Cor. 12:11). Jesus described the Spirit as One who had *knowledge* when He said that He would teach us all things and guide us into all truth (John 14:26; 16:13). One cannot teach truth unless one has knowledge of the truth. The Holy Spirit is an individual Who can feel the *emotions* of being grieved, insulted, and quenched (Eph. 4:30; Heb. 10:29; 1 Thes. 5:19).

When Jesus was preparing His disciples for His departure, He promised that He would not leave them as orphans because He would send another Helper to take His place (John 14:16-18). Anyone who is not enjoying the same caliber of a relationship with the Holy Spirit that the disciples had with Jesus is needlessly living as a spiritual orphan.

4) **Misconception: The Holy Spirit never speaks about Himself, and it is wrong to include Him in our expressions of adoration during worship.**

The Scriptures, church history, and our hymnals contradict this doctrine. It was the Holy Spirit who inspired the men who wrote the Scriptures. If the Spirit-inspired references to the Holy Spirit were deleted from the Bible, it would be a much thinner book. One would be hard-pressed to find a greater number of biblical references describing the nature and function of any other member of the Godhead that would outnumber those that relate directly to the Holy Spirit.

During the fourth century AD, theologians met in council to unravel the confusion of heretics who were denying the separate identities of the three persons of the Godhead. The deity of Jesus and the personhood of the Holy Spirit were the primary issues at hand. The council released the Nicene Creed as the confession of clarification. It relates these truths about the Godhead: "We believe in one God; And in one Lord Jesus Christ, the Son of God, begotten of the Father, light of light, very God of very God, begotten and not made, being of one substance with the Father; And we believe in the Holy Ghost, the Lord and giver of life, who proceedeth from the Father, who with the Father and the Son, is worshipped and glorified, who spake by the prophets."

Our hymn books are filled with song titles and hymn verses that glorify the Holy Spirit and prayers of invocation that are set to music to invite His presence. The following lines are examples from some much beloved hymns: "Come, gracious Spirit, heavenly Dove…Praise ye the Spirit, comforter of Israel…Spirit of God descend upon my heart…Spirit of the living God fall afresh on me…Sweet Holy Spirit, sweet heavenly Dove, stay right here with us, filling us with Your love."

5) **Misconception: The Lord is satisfied to make His presence known through the unobtrusive voice of His Spirit within our hearts. The Bible does not encourage the concept that His presence can be felt physically. We need faith, not feelings.**

The Scriptures, church history, and contemporary experience do not support this misconception. The Scriptures reveal that it is God's nature to punctuate His will for us with exhibitions of attention-getting power; although in the following instances from the Bible, He would have been no less God had He been mystically subtle rather than miraculously demonstrative.

When Elijah was hiding from Jezebel in the wilderness cave, God chose to announce His "still small voice" instructions with fire from heaven, an earthquake, and a windstorm so powerful that it burst boulders and uprooted trees. It would have certainly been more "environmentally friendly" had He limited His activity to a hardly perceptible whisper during Elijah's morning devotions. Apparently, He enjoys episodes wherein He has the assurance that He has our undivided attention when He speaks (1 Kings 19:11-12). The disciples rejoiced and prayed in one accord when Peter and John were released from the Pharisees. A simple "amen" from one of the elders would have been sufficient to conclude the meeting, but God made the occasion memorable by shaking the entire building (Acts 4:23-31).

The pre-incarnate Son of God appeared to Jacob as a man and wrestled with him all night long. Surely, if all the Lord wanted to do was change Jacob's name to Israel and give him a limp, He could have done so in an instant. However, it seems that the Redeemer has a propensity that caused Him to long for an opportunity to interact with His creation (Gen. 32:24-30).

Along this same line, the words "fell/fallen" in Greek mean to embrace with affection, or to seize more or less violently. Peter needed to prove to the Jewish saints that it was kosher for him to have taken the message of salvation to the Gentiles. His defense was that the Holy Spirit had *fallen* upon them just as He had on Jews on the day of Pentecost. Peter was saying, "I personally heard them speaking in tongues and saw evidence that the Holy Spirit fell on them [was giving them tangible hugs of His affection], just as He did when He first touched us" (Acts 11:15-18).

There is a current global outpouring of the Holy Spirit that is referred to as the "renewal" or the "Father's blessing." In this move, God is emphasizing the fact that He has physiologically designed us with the capacity to be physically reminded of His spiritual omnipresence. In meeting halls of every description and denomination, saints and sinners are confronted with something in the atmosphere that seems distinctively holy. As this awesome, invigorating force descends, people begin to experience physiological responses. It is not unusual for some to spontaneously shriek with outcries of repentance. Others break forth into long episodes of laughter wherein mature people sound like joyful children who have never known a day of responsibility or emotional stress. Many begin to tremble with what appears to be spasms from light jolts of heavenly electricity. Scores can be seen gently collapsing to the floor as their physical strength melts under the weight of God's manifest glory. Hundreds of others simply stand and soak in the current of Spirit-breathed energy, which they can feel subtly pulsating through them. Thousands who attend these services are touched with varying intensities of the feelings of God's nearness. Many subsequently discover that the Lord has done significant inward works, freeing them of habitual sins, dysfunctional attitudes, and physical ailments.

Acts 3:19-21 implies that as God's people repent of their independence, He, in turn, continually grants them cycles of refreshing. He refreshes us for the purpose of restoration until all the things that He has for us are restored to us. The word "restore" means to put back into place the things that have been missing from their rightful place.

Church history commentaries reveal that *every major revival* has had the accompanying signs of physiological manifestations. They also indicate that when leaders, whose congregations had been blessed by the revivals, began to publicly dismiss the value of the accompanying manifestations, it inevitably signaled the decline of those movements. One could easily conclude that the reason for this is because God's people have failed to grasp that He wanted to restore these signs to us permanently.

It could be that Hilary of Poitiers, a 4th century theologian, discerned correctly what our expectations should reflect when he wrote: "When we receive the Holy Spirit we are made drunk. Because out of us, as a source, various streams of grace flow, the prophet prays that the Lord will inebriate us. The prophet wants the same persons to be made drunk, and filled to all fullness with the divine gifts, so that their generation may be multiplied."

The manifestations are far more than mere temporary tokens of God's presence. They should be embraced and encouraged as permanent tangible indicators of the Lord's abiding presence. We need to continually say: "More, Lord!"

Chapter 3

Satan And Demons

When I was 25, I was introduced to the Charismatic world. It was then that I began to come to the realization that there were significant areas wherein my spiritual education, though good, had been incomplete. One area in which I was uninformed was that of the reality of Satan and demons. My discovery of this realm was both blessed and precarious. I was blessed as lifelong bondages were stripped from my character. However, my spiritual walk became precarious when I became so caught up in the novelty of this realm that I could hardly think or talk of anything else. I saw the evidence of the demonic everywhere, all of the time. The Lord graciously rescued me by giving me a revelation that others have since found helpful.

The world of Satan and his demonic hordes could be compared to the germ-filled atmosphere in which we live. Innumerable forms of dangerous germs exist in the air around us. Our awareness of them does not increase or diminish the reality of their existence. No one, other than a hypochondriac, becomes preoccupied with the potential for the presence of germs. Most people trust in inoculations, personal hygiene, and the intermittent use of disinfectants to keep them out of harm's way. On the rare occasions when bacterial germs do attack, they respond to the proper antibiotics and then run their course.

Satanic entities exist, and they have the potential to be dangerous; however, Christians need not become overly concerned about them. The Spirit of God and the blood of Jesus have inoculated us (1 Cor. 6:11; 2 Tim. 4:18). The disinfectants of regular Christian fellowship and a reasonable devotional life cleanse the atmosphere around us (1 Jn. 1:7; 2:14). If the enemy does attack us, we can banish his presence through the brief regimen of the antibiotics of spiritual warfare (Rev. 12:11).

1) **Misconception: Satan and his demons live in hell.**

Hell is a place of torment prepared for Satan and his evil cohorts. It is a prison of torturous pain in which no one would choose to live, and from which none are free to leave. Presently, it is the abode of the spirits of the unrighteous who rejected salvation through Christ (Luke 16:22-24). In addition, there are a relatively small number of fallen angels consigned to chains in hell (2 Pet. 2:4; Jude 1:6). Satan will not be consigned there until the millennial reign of Christ (Matt. 8:28-29; Rev. 20:1-3). He will be released for a short time afterward and will attempt to deceive the inhabitants of the earth to join an insurrection against the kingdom of God. This attempt will fail, and Satan and his rebels will be totally defeated in the battle of Armageddon. Their punishment will be eternal damnation in hell's lake of fire (Rev. 20:3-10).

2) **Misconception: Fallen angels and demons are synonymous terms.**

Demons are evil entities of a different order than fallen angels. Jesus said that when evil spirits are cast out of a person, they walk through dry, desolate places seeking rest (Matt. 12:43-44). They are earthbound, spiritual personalities that are restless because they crave a human body through which to express their depraved desires. If they cannot find a person to inhabit, they will temporarily accept the alternative of an animal (Mark 5:13).

There is no biblical record that indicates an incidence where a fallen angel possessed the body of a person, while the Scriptures are resplendent with cases of demons infesting humans. Fallen angels have spiritual bodies, and some have wings. Satan was one of the winged variety called cherubs before he rebelled against God and was cast out of the third heaven where God dwells (1 Kings 6:24; Ezek. 28:13:15; Isa. 14:12).

Satan and his fallen angels dwell in an area called the second heaven. They have the ability to descend and ascend between heaven and earth. The foundation for the terminology of first and second heavens is biblical deductive reasoning. The Apostle Paul said that he was taken up into the third heaven and given revelations from God (2 Cor. 12:2). If one labels something as third, logic dictates that there is a first and a second. Satan was cast out of heaven, yet he still remains the prince of the power of the air (Eph. 2:2). He and his fallen angels operate from heavenly principalities (Eph. 6:12). If they no longer dwell in God's third heaven, but yet they still reside in the heavens, it could cause one to conclude that they live in the first and the second heavens. The evil angel that attempted to thwart the angel's efforts to bring answers to Daniel's prayers met him in the heavens over Persia (Dan. 10:10-14,20). It is apparent that Satan's kingdom has a form of military order. He and his fallen angels serve as officers in the heavenly realms that marshal demons on the earthly level to harass mankind.

3) Misconception: Satan is a completely defeated idiot. He is just a harmless pussycat.

It is unwise and unscriptural to refer to the archenemy of the purposes of God in a flippant manner (Jude 1:8-9). Through His death on the cross and victorious resurrection, Jesus did defeat Satan. However, before His crucifixion, He told Peter that the devil had plans to sift him as wheat (Luke 22:31). He was speaking of Peter's denial of Christ on the night of his betrayal and his subsequent temporary abandonment of the ministry. This clearly recognizes that Satan would continue to have elements of power after the resurrection of Jesus. Thirty years later, Paul concurred with this when he told the Roman Christians that Satan would be shortly subdued under their feet (Rom. 16:20). The Devil still roams about like a roaring lion seeking those whom he may devour (1 Pet. 5:8-9). A toothless pussycat cannot claw into people's lives with enslaving addictions, spousal abuse, and devastating illnesses.

He was defeated by Christ, but each Christian is challenged to make that victory viable in their experience by being vigilant to resist him in faith. We can overcome Satan as we testify to the power of the blood of the Lamb in our lives (Rev. 12:10-11).

4) Superstition: You must be careful when attending Christian charismatic healing services because the servants of Satan also have the power to heal people.

During His earthly ministry, Jesus went about doing good and healing all of those that were oppressed by the devil (Acts 10:38). The explicit implications are that sicknesses are often related to various forms of satanic influence. When Jesus was accused of casting out demons through the power of Satan, His response was that a kingdom divided against itself could not stand. He was saying that it would be counterproductive for Satan to cast out Satan (Matt. 12:25-26). Based upon this fact, it is highly improbable that Satan would allow his ambassadors to alleviate suffering that he initiated.

God, in His mercy, has designed the human body with the capacity to heal itself. When a sickly person is given hope for healing, certain secretions begin to circulate through their body, activating the body's potential to heal itself. When it appears that a servant of Satan has effected a healing, it is far more likely that they are taking the credit for the blessing of this natural physiological phenomena. The patient, for whom they supposedly performed the cure, simply was encouraged by the hope of healing through their enchantments. Taking a placebo claimed to be a miracle pill would routinely bring the same positive results.

Chapter 4

The Baptism in the Holy Spirit

Most everyone in the various camps of God's people would agree that our tensions over the experience of the baptism in the Holy Spirit are less than ideal. The ideal would be that we were all in agreement on basic doctrinal issues. In 1981 I heard a prophetic utterance through Derek Prince that has helped settle my spirit about the actuality of these tensions. He has been my friend and a ministry colleague for over 30 years. He is a Greek and Latin scholar who held a professorship of Philosophy at King's College, Cambridge, in Britain.

The gist of Derek's prophetic utterance was the following: In your journey there are two situations—the actual and the ideal. To be mature is to see the ideal and live with the actual. To fail is to accept the actual and reject the ideal. To accept only that which is ideal and refuse the actual is immature. Do not criticize the actual because you have seen the ideal. Do not reject the ideal because you see the actual. Maturity is to live with the actual but to hold to the ideal.

The following are common misconceptions about the baptism in the Holy Spirit and biblical answers to them.

1) **Misconception: We are automatically filled with the Holy Spirit when we are born again so there is no need to seek a subsequent experience of being baptized in the Spirit.**

Anyone who has been saved has had an encounter with the Holy Spirit. At conversion, the Holy Spirit moves upon us and we are born again by the Spirit (John 3:3-8). This is not synonymous with the baptism of the Holy Spirit. In the new birth, we receive the Holy Spirit as He gives us newness of life. Subsequently through the baptism in the Holy Spirit, we can be empowered for Christian service. When Philip the evangelist preached Christ in Samaria, he did not consider his job complete until the new converts had been baptized in water, filled with the Holy Spirit, and exposed to the miraculous realities of divine healing and deliverance (Acts 8:5-8,12,14-17). In those days, the sacrament of water baptism was not administered to the unsaved. The text says that after their water baptism, the Holy Spirit had not yet fallen upon any of them. Therefore, Philip sent for Peter and John to journey from Jerusalem to lay hands on them that they might receive the Holy Spirit. If salvation and the baptism in the Holy Spirit were synonymous, the apostles made a needless journey.

2) **Misconception: Through the baptism in the Holy Spirit you received all of the Holy Spirit that you will ever need. If you want more, just tap into the reservoir that resides within you.**

The New Testament indicates that the early disciples not only had an initial experience of being baptized in the Holy Spirit but also had many subsequent infillings (Acts 4:8,31; 13:9; 13:52). The word in the Greek for "filled" means a reduplication of that which has been done previously. There would be no need for the texts to emphasize that people were *refilled* if it was the common understanding that one's initial baptism in the Holy Spirit kept one filled for a lifetime. If one has been filled and needs a subsequent refilling, the indications are that the vessel leaks. The pressures of everyday life drain all of us. It would behoove us all to seek the Lord for intermittent fresh infillings of the Holy Spirit.

3) **Misconception: I do not prophesy, pray for the sick, or speak in tongues, but I know that I have the baptism in the Holy Spirit because I have the gift of love.**

Love is an admirable quality that Christians owe as a debt to everyone whom they encounter (Rom. 13:8). It is an aspect of the *fruit of the Spirit* rather than a spiritual gift, as there are no biblical references that label it as a gift (Gal. 5:22). We are exhorted to pursue love and to desire spiritual gifts (1 Cor. 14:1). The reason for this is that even though both love and spiritual gifts are spiritual abilities of different kinds, they work hand in hand. It could be said that love on its own is a lonely noun. When love is expressed *through* the activation of a gift of the Spirit on behalf of someone in need, it becomes an active verb. For instance, a person could verbally express love to another who was sick and in financial need. The words might be comforting, but they are incomplete in satisfying the depth of the suffering person's need to experience a tangible expression of God's love. Then suppose that the person who offered the sentiment had the gift of giving and wrote a check to cover all of their medical bills (Rom. 12:8; 1 Jn. 3:17-18). At this juncture, the love of God would be translated from a vague spiritual concept to a living testimony in the needy person's life.

Chapter 5

The Gifts of the Holy Spirit

The Scriptures offer no indication of the style in which the gifts of the Spirit were administered by the members of the early church. I have concluded that the Lord leaves a lot up to our personal comfort zones as to how we prefer to minister and what ministry style of others attracts us enough to make it easy for us to receive from them. In this regard, my experience has led me to believe that theatrics in the exercise of the gifts hinders many from welcoming ministry. We can be reasonably sure that Jesus did not put His hand to His brow as He concentrated to receive a word of knowledge about the Samaritan woman's marital history (John 4:17-18). It is equally doubtful that the apostles led those who came for healing in a unified countdown to the precise moment that Peter's healing shadow would be the longest and bless the optimum number of seekers (Acts 5:15-16).

Generally, people are more impressed with ministers who present themselves as ordinary and then do extraordinary acts, than they are with those who present themselves in an extraordinary manner before they have demonstrated noteworthy acts. An example of this happened while I was golfing one day. I had joined a foursome that included two women who were LPGA professionals. During the round, two things became obvious. The women were romantically involved with one another, and one was nursing a shoulder injury. Midway through the round, she excused her poor play because of pain. I asked if I could attempt to help her. She was not aware that I was a minister and nodded yes with a puzzled expression. I did not adjust my voice to pulpit tremor and request her repentance from her abominable lifestyle. Neither did I purpose for my hand to quiver as I touched her. I simply smiled at her and laid my hand upon the problem shoulder. Several holes later, she couldn't hold back her curiosity any longer and burst out, "When you touched me, heat went through my shoulder and all the pain is gone. Who are you and what did you do to me?" I explained that I was a pastor and that I had inwardly prayed for her healing as I touched her. She expressed surprised gratitude and subtly hinted that she was relieved that I had not gone through the theatrics she would have anticipated from a faith healer. Since that time, she and her partner have welcomed conversations with me. The Lord will harvest them in His time.

1) **Misconception: The Bible tells us that the gifts of the Holy Spirit will cease. The portion of the Gospel of Mark which says that signs such as laying hands on the sick and speaking in tongues will follow is not in the most reliable manuscripts.**

Those who make these claims do so in order to discount the legitimacy of spiritual gifts for the contemporary church. Normally, the same people would strongly assert that they believe the Bible to be the infallible Word of God. Candid consistency should cause them to believe that the men who chose the books that were to be canonized were just as infallibly inspired as the men who originally penned the manuscripts. They would be chagrined at the way their Bibles would be altered if the same texts that do not contain Mark 16:17-20 had been used to canonize the Scriptures. Most of these manuscripts leave out the following portions of the Bible: Gen. 1-46; Psa. 105-137; Heb. 9:14; 13:25, 1 & 2 Timothy, Titus, Philemon, and the entire book of Revelations.

The portion of Scripture that says that spiritual gifts such as prophecy and tongues will vanish is 1 Cor. 12:8-13. The context reveals that this will not occur until we see the Lord face to face, and we know Him as completely as He knows us. Believers will not achieve this until the Second Coming (1 John 3:2).

2) Misconception: There are nine gifts of the Holy Spirit.

Actually, there are at least 28! The Holy Spirit functions as the divine administrator of all the blessings that the Father and the Son wish to impart to the Church. There are three *redemptive* gifts. They are: repentance, righteousness, and eternal life (2 Tim. 2:25; Rom. 5:17; 6:23). There are nine *gifts of the Spirit* that can be operated by any spirit-filled believer in Christian gatherings for the common good (1 Cor. 12:7-11). These are: words of wisdom and knowledge, faith, healing, miracles, prophecy, distinguishing of spirits, tongues for the assembly, and the interpretation of tongues.

There are fourteen *gifts of anointed ministers* that God appoints in the church. These would include: apostles, prophets, teachers, miracle workers, those with the gifts of healing, helps, administration, those who regularly speak in tongues and those who interpret those tongues for the edification of the church, exhortation, financial giving, mercy, pastors, and evangelists (1 Cor. 12:28-30; Rom. 12:6-8; Eph. 4:11). There are some people that are like the Apostle Paul and have the gift of *celibacy* (1 Cor. 7:7-8). Then there is the gift of *devotional tongues* that all who have the baptism in the Holy Spirit possess. Paul preferred not to speak in tongues publicly, but privately he claimed that he spoke in tongues more than anyone else did (Rom. 8:26; 1 Cor. 14:15,18-19). The combined total of all of these gifts comes to 28.

3) Misconception: The gift of tongues is inferior to the gift of prophecy.

This argument is often used by some people to devalue the gift of speaking in tongues in contemporary experience. They build their stand around two verses in Paul's first letter to the Corinthians. One verse speaks about desiring the best gifts, and the other says that one who prophesies is greater than one who speaks in tongues (1 Cor. 12:31; 14:5). Their reasoning is faulty because Paul was not addressing the practice of praying in tongues during one's private devotions. He was talking about the use of tongues in public assemblies where the uninformed could be in attendance (1 Cor. 14:23). Paul qualified his statement that greater was one who prophesies than one who speaks in tongues by adding the words "unless he interprets that the whole church might be edified" (1 Cor. 14:5). In so doing, he put the public use of tongues, coupled with a following interpretation, on the same plane of value as prophecy. In the following verse, he gave tongues and interpretation another promotion. He used the word "unless" again. The context implies that the interpretation of tongues can bring revelation, knowledge, prophecy, and teaching (1 Cor. 14:6).

4) Misconception: Our intercessory prayer group was praying for our church and the Lord showed us that our pastor had a spirit of manipulation. Several of us are considering leaving the church as we do not want to be under the influence of a controlling spirit.

If a revelation of this nature occurred, it might be a manifestation of the gift of the Holy Spirit known as discerning or distinguishing of spirits (1 Cor. 12:10). All gifts of the Holy Spirit that come forth are to be for the good of all concerned (1 Cor. 12:7). This means that if it were accurate, it would profit not only those who received it but also the person to which it referred. It is unscriptural and unfair for people to judge a person on the basis of a subjective revelation that has not been evaluated for its accuracy (1 Cor. 14:29). This would require that the individual who received it approach the one to whom it pertained in humility to discuss its accuracy (Gal. 6:1-3; Matt. 18:15-17). If it was perceived as accurate, that person must be offered the opportunity to repent and change. The revelation gifts can be a wonderful source of insight and blessing if they are acted upon with wisdom. They can be equally hurtful if they are not properly evaluated for their objective accuracy.

Chapter 6

Those Who Minister

The laymen of New Testament times functioned with a high level of proficiency in spiritual gifts. When compared to them, we live in a sub-normal atmosphere. Today, anyone who functions in what was once considered common gifting is perceived as unique. This causes some to overestimate the level of their gifting and to quit their jobs to enter the ministry as a means of livelihood. Many of them are later forced to abandon the ministry due to the emotional stress that comes from financial pressures. The fact that a person loves the Lord and can flow in spiritual gifts does not mean God has appointed them for vocational ministry. Every Christian has spiritual gifts, but not all are called to be ministry gifts to the Body of Christ (1 Cor. 12:28-30).

During the tenure of my public ministry, we have seen over 40 people who had once sat in the pews pursue and thrive in various fields of full-time ministry. Beyond their ability to flow in their gifting in a public setting, I have used a practical biblical criteria to help them discern if they were called to vocational ministry. The Word tells us that those who are called to the Gospel should live by the Gospel. It implies that these will be graced with divine attestation in a manner similar to Aaron. His wooden rod budded, and the other men's rods, who were pressing for recognition, did not (1 Cor. 9:11-14; Heb. 5:4; Num. 17:3-5). Those who are graced for full-time service will draw unsolicited financial support, when others who are equally gifted in spiritual gifts will not. It has been my experience that those who are called will so bless people with their gifting that those who receive these spiritual blessings will regularly endeavor to reciprocate with material blessings. If there is not a significant flow of finances coming one's way prior to full-time ministry, it might be a good indication that it will be negligible later.

1) **Superstition: The Lord will not use an unclean vessel.**

There are no biblical or contemporary indicators that the anointing of God is a conditional loan (Rom. 11:29). During our generation, many Christians have agonized in disappointment and embarrassment as some of our chief media champions have been exposed in the grips of bondage to grievous sins. It should be noted that it was the exposure of their sins rather than the commission of sins that tempered their functioning as servants of God.

The Apostle Paul thanked God for the members of the Corinthian church and commended them for possessing all the spiritual gifts even though gross immorality was common among them (1 Cor. 1:1-8; 5:1). He called for them to refrain from dragging Christ through the mire of their immoralities by fleeing from their sins (1 Cor. 6:15-20). In a later letter, he admonished all Christians to cleanse themselves of filthiness of flesh and spirit as they pressed toward experiential holiness (2 Cor. 7:1). The Lord does not condone sin, but He does use imperfect people to touch others with His mercy.

2) **Misconception: Women should not be allowed to teach or to hold key places of leadership within the church because Paul said, "And I do not permit a woman to teach or to have authority over a man, but to be in silence" (1 Tim. 2:11).**

This position is spiritual thievery because historically it has robbed the church of gifted ministries that could have been of great benefit. It is erroneous from several perspectives. It is unwise to build a doctrine on a single text that has been lifted from the context of the verses around it. The context of this passage strongly indicates that Paul was referring to a wife's proper relationship with *her husband* and not the church. The church is not mentioned in the passage. There is reference made to Adam and Eve, and they were husband and wife. Childbearing is also mentioned in these verses, which is a function of a married woman. It is helpful to note that the word used for "woman" can indicate a woman generically or a wife specifically, depending on the context in which it is used. Here it indicates a wife as the word for "man" means one who is a husband.

In addition, the phrase "or to have authority over a man, but to be in silence" is worthy of examination. "To have authority over" literally means *to act of one's self*; and figuratively, it means *to dominate*. The word translated as silence does not indicate muteness but rather *tranquility*. A reasonable interpretation of the gist of 1 Timothy 2:11-13 might read: "A wife is to follow her husband's instructions in a tranquil, submissive manner. I do not allow a wife to constantly dominate her husband through overbearing directive instructions. A wife should tranquilly keep in mind that it was Eve rather than Adam who was first deceived."

Women did play key roles in the public ministry of the first century church and its apostolic teams. Paul called the following women his fellow workers: Priscilla, Euodia, Syntyche, and Phoebe (Rom. 16:1-3; Philip. 4:2-3). The same word that is translated as fellow workers is used of the men: Timothy, Aquila, Clement, Mark, Aristarchus, Demas, and Luke (Rom. 16:3,21; Philip. 4:3; Phile. 1:24). It appears that men and women shared equal responsibilities in the ministry.

There are a number of passages that indicate that men did learn spiritual truths from women and nothing can be learned if it was not previously taught. The team of Priscilla and Aquila explained the Gospel to Apollos. If Aquila was the only one actively involved, Priscilla's name would have been unnecessary (Acts 18:26). Women did pray and prophesy in mixed gatherings of the early church (Acts 21:9; 1 Cor. 11:5). Paul said that all of those in the assembly could prophesy one by one, that all may learn (1 Cor. 14:31). This would include the women who were present. The men who listened could not learn anything unless there was an element of teaching in the prophecies that both men and women brought forth.

3) **Misconception: People from divorced backgrounds should be excluded from positions of spiritual leadership. The Bible tells us that pastors and deacons are to be the husbands of one wife. Those who have had previous marriages simply do not qualify.**

This is a complicated issue that has caused many servants of God to be thwarted in their ministries. Simply stated, any person who has biblical grounds for divorce has an equal right to remarry. In situations where a spouse violated the marriage covenant through adultery or left the marriage because the other has become a Christian, the believer is not bound to the marriage (Matt. 19:9; 1 Cor. 7:15). There is no cloud hanging over them that would prevent them from entering spiritual leadership if they were called to do so. Many commentators concur that when Paul made the qualification that a leader must be the husband of one wife, he meant one wife at a time (1 Tim. 3:2,12). The reason for this was that polygamy was a common practice in the Mediterranean world. Many of those who were spiritually astute enough to be leaders were disqualified because they were bogged down with too many family responsibilities to really care for the people of God.

4) Misconception: My spouse is holding me back spiritually, and I am praying about a divorce. It would free me to attend church services more frequently and provide me with increased opportunities to function in my spiritual gifting.

This reasoning exposes a misconception about the nature of the Christian life and underestimates the extent of God's providential care. The Christian life is not designed to revolve around religious meetings. The ultimate test of spiritual maturity is not how one performs while under the anointing in public ministry. In reality, the Bible devotes relatively little attention to how one is to operate in spiritual gifts while in church. It primarily focuses on how we are to flow in the love and discipline of God in our interpersonal relationships, families, and vocations. The level of one's spiritual maturity is reflected in their ability to exemplify the virtues of the Holy Spirit in the stresses of everyday life (Gal. 5:22-23). If we have been unable to import the peace and benevolent authority of God into our families and vocations, we have little to export to church services and to the world.

God understands that those who are married will be limited in the amount of time and energy that they can devote to pursuits that are considered overtly religious (1 Cor. 7:32-34). He endorses marriage by extending ministry beyond the perimeters of church life. A wife who peacefully endures her husband's complaints about Christians or a husband who forgives his wife's manipulative tactics are engaged in activities that are no less spiritual than praying for the sick or preaching (1 Pet. 3:1-7; Eph. 5:25-28; Col. 3:19). The primary ministry of those who are married to unconverted or uncooperative spouses is to draw them to Christ through their exemplary faith, patience, and love. The presence of the believer in the marriage sanctifies the unbeliever for the redemptive purposes of God (1 Cor. 7:14-17).

Paul admonished those who were born-again slaves not to be concerned about the limiting nature of slavery. He insinuated that even a slave was free to do all for which the Lord had called them (1 Cor. 7:20-22). If slavery cannot restrict a person's spiritual effectiveness, a less than ideal marriage situation is powerless to do so. The pursuits of spiritual interest and Christian service are never legitimate motivations for divorce (1 Cor. 7:10-13,27).

5) **Superstition: Ministers who use non-Christian resources and terminology to convey biblical truths should be suspect of New Age contamination.**

People who hold this position might find sitting under the ministries of the Apostle Paul and Apollos disconcerting. In two New Testament passages, Paul quoted Epimenides and Aratus (Tit. 1:12-13; Acts 17:28). Both of these men were heathen poets and soothsayers who lived hundreds of years before Christ. The name *Apollos* means "belonging to Apollo." He was the Greek and Roman deity attributed to having the power to grant inspiration for healing, music, poetry, and prophecy. Any minister whose message expresses the reliability of God's Word, and a character that bears witness that he has embraced the cross of Christ, should not come under condemnation for his background or the secular terms that he might use in order to help the unbelievers come to understand the Gospel.

6) Misconception: If you had more faith, you would have received your healing when God's man of faith and power laid hands on you.

This insensitive statement misplaces the responsibility for the faith needed to accomplish a healing. Jesus commended people for having the faith sufficient to receive healing simply on their confident confessions that they believed that He could provide it. A kinder posture might be to place the primary weight for faith on the minister attempting to administer healing rather than the intended recipient (1 Cor. 12:28; Rom. 12:6). But in the end, it is God's decision whether or not a healing will take place. We may not understand His reasons until we see Him face to face.

Chapter 7

The Ministry

One of my chief joys is to see ministers flowing in their gifting, thereby blessing those to whom they minister. Those who consistently do so are those who do not rely on past successes but rather regularly sit at the Lord's feet to receive fresh bread for His sheep. Ministers who attempt to circumvent this discipline often find that they are ensnared in a boringly predictable routine. When this occurs, everyone involved comes away unfulfilled.

If an itinerant minister is not receiving fresh bread before he attempts to minister to God's people, the deceptive subtleties of the routine begin to emerge. Each time he ministers, the only things that change are the date, the location, and the faces in front of him. The effectiveness of his canned messages has been dissipated because they may not be appropriate for successive congregations. It is not unusual for even supposedly spontaneous prophetic words to fall into a predictable "nightly rut," giving the same exhortations to similarly appearing persons in different venues. The only antidote for these pitfalls is fresh bread from the Master. Any minister who waits before the Lord and disciplines himself to avoid familiar verbiage can be assured that when he opens his mouth the Lord will fill it (Psa. 145:15; Prov. 15:23; Psa. 81:10).

1) Superstition: If I get serious about working for God, I will be subjected to a relentless backlash of attacks from the enemy.

If this premise were factual, it would be vindicated by a comparison of heathen nations with those nations where the Gospel is proclaimed by the Lord's servants. Satan would have exempted the citizens of such nations as Haiti and India from attacks, and so they should be enjoying more blessings than the inhabitants of Christianized nations. To the contrary, there is far greater liberty for progress in the nations where Christians are serving as lights as they labor for the Lord. The devil does not allow those who cower from him to live trouble free, healthy, prosperous lives. He seeks opportunities to disrupt the lives of everyone, everywhere, all of the time. But Christians have an advantage; he will flee from those who resist him in faith (1 Pet. 5:8-9). Believers are uniquely equipped with offensive weapons to overcome Satan. In the book of Revelation, the Apostle John predicted that Satan would be overcome as Christians testified to the power of the blood of the Lamb (Rev. 12:11). In his first epistle, he commended the young men who had defeated Satan through the power of the Word abiding in them (1 Jn. 2:14).

2) Superstition: Never lay hands on a sinful or demonized person because you might experience a transfer of spirits.

The text that is used to validate the teaching that sinful behavior and demons can be transferred to a Christian who lays hands upon an afflicted person is 1 Timothy 5:22. However, the general context for this verse is that Timothy had been left in

Ephesus to ordain leaders. Paul's admonition was that these appointments not be made in haste, because Timothy would be responsible for the conduct of those he ordained. The Living Bible renders this text: "Never be in a hurry about choosing a pastor; you may overlook his sins, and it will look as if you approve of them. Be sure that you yourself stay away from all sin." The truth is, Jesus was the master of deliverance, and He did lay hands on those who had evil spirits (Lk. 13:10-13). It stands to reason that if the Holy Spirit honors a minister's faith by expelling an evil spirit from a person's personality, He would certainly protect that minister from the transfer of demonic infestation.

3) Misconception: Inevitable curses will be passed to each successive generation if there has been an occultist, a member of the Masons, or a promiscuous fornicator in a past generation. Anyone who wants to find complete freedom in the Lord must examine their family histories and repent for the specific sins of past generations.

There are scriptural references and isolated contemporary instances that seemingly vindicate this teaching. It is undeniable that generational sins and their attached penalties of poverty, sickness, and relational disharmony can pass from one generation to the next. The difficulty lies in presuming the *probability* of generational curses being the source of a person's problems rather than a *remote possibility* for them.

The cross of Christ is the generational curse breaker. When Jesus was crucified, He became a curse for us and took the penalty for every form of sin that our ancestors or we committed (Gal. 3:13-14). One of the benefits of becoming new creations in Christ is that we do not have to bear the penalties for our forefather's sins (Jer. 31:29-33). The majority of believers can safely rely on the atoning death of Jesus without fearing reprisals for the sins of past generations. In the rare instances wherein perplexities stubbornly resist the routine Christian sacraments of prayer for healing and blessings, it may be viable to specifically renounce the sins of former generations. Whenever a person does this, they are entering the eternal realm of the Spirit where they simply update their faith in what Jesus did for them at Calvary. Following this act, neither they nor future generations who find faith in Christ will have to repeatedly repent of those specific offenses.

4) Misconception: Sinful, dysfunctional behavior is inevitably caused by a dysfunctional family environment. Problem people come from problem families and troubled neighborhoods.

These widely accepted generalizations are as unscriptural as they are unfair. The fact is that Adam and Eve were the products of a single parent home that was by no means dysfunctional. Their environment was perfect, yet they still made bad choices and blamed others for their failures (Gen. 2:6-12). Cain was not overcome with gang peer pressure when he became filled with depressive jealousy and killed his brother Abel (Gen. 4:5-8). Although King David was described as a man after God's own heart, he had one son who raped his sister and another who killed his brother and overthrew the throne of his father (Acts 13:22; 2 Sam. 13:1-19,28; 15:13-14). Extremely dysfunctional families can intensify the possibility that their children will suffer from dysfunctional issues. Conversely, it is not unusual for good families to have children with equal intensities of aberrant behavior. In these instances, the ancient biblical solution was that the offender, not his parents, was stoned. This alternative is not suggested, but it was undoubtedly effective in punctuating the concept that we are all solely responsible for our actions.

It could be that the Church has unwittingly overdosed on humanistic, psychological methods to address issues that are primarily spiritual. Psychological terms can be helpful in defining the ills of the human soul, but they fall short on providing cures for them. Perhaps in our good intentioned efforts to build people's self-esteem, we forget how very far man fell through original sin. The human heart is desperately wicked (Jer. 17:9). The only sure cure is salvation through faith in Jesus coupled with the discipline of embracing the cross and crucifying the desires of our flesh and minds (1 Cor. 1:18; Luke 9:23-24; Gal. 5:24).

5) Misconception: The Holy Spirit is a gentleman. He would never override a person's free will or inspire them to do anything that might be embarrassing.

This characterization is commonly offered to make God the Holy Spirit more appealing to those who might be apprehensive about His work. The difficulty is that the God of the Bible has never obligated Himself to operate solely within our comfort zones. It is likely that the prophet Isaiah initially felt a little awkward when he was inspired to prophesy while naked for three years (Isa. 20:2-3). It is doubtful that Ananias and his wife Sapphira would have opted for divine execution had they been given a choice in the matter (Acts 5:1-10). Elymas the magician did not welcome the inconvenience when Paul invoked God to smite him with temporary blindness (Acts 13:8-11). The person of the Holy Spirit is described as a wind. No man can domesticate His velocity. He blows *how* He wants to, *when* He wants to, and *upon whom* He desires.

6) Misconception: I am hesitant to pray for the sick because if they are not healed they might become so disappointed that they lose their confidence in the Lord.

Often when a person makes a new acquaintance with a medical doctor, they inquire about what they do for a living. A common response is, "I practice medicine." When doctors take the Hippocratic oath, they pledge that they will treat patients to the best of their ability. They see themselves as obligated to make genuine efforts to see that those who come to them are restored to health. All the while, they understand that there are no guarantees because they are *practicing* their craft.

Those who are believers in the Lord Jesus Christ don't take an oath, but we do have a direct command to lay hands on the sick and see them recover (Mark 16:17-18). Just as the doctors have an obligation to practice medicine, we have an obligation to practice our faith. The laying on of hands is our responsibility. The subsequent recovery is dependent upon unknown variable factors between the patient and God. In reality, most people who are ill greatly appreciate the efforts of those who attempt to see them recover whether it be by medicine or faith. It is rare to find a seriously ill person who stops seeking medical help because numerous doctors failed. Most will continue seeking out the physicians in the hope of eventual healing. It would be even more rare for an ill person to lose hope in God just because a mere human failed to secure a miraculous healing on their behalf.

7) **Misconception: We prayed for a Christian's healing, and he died; but nonetheless, God healed him. He is now perfectly whole in heaven.**

This position may serve as a temporary consolation for our souls, but it does not plumb the cry for truth that resides in our spirits. The Holy Spirit within us teaches us and reveals truth to us (John 16:13; 1 John 2:27). The inspired truth of the Word of God and common logic nullify this argument. If it were true, every Christian who died from illness would have been healed regardless of whether or not they received prayer, and so the word "heal" would lose its significance. Furthermore, a forensic scientist could exhume their remains and identify the disease that caused their deaths. If a person was divinely healed, his/her body would bear no evidence that would identify sickness as the cause of death.

When people die, they are instantly in the presence of the Lord in soul and spirit (2 Cor. 5:8); however, their bodies will remain in the ground until the rapture. At that time, their physical bodies will take on a glorified form, free from all of the traumas of disease. Their glorified bodies will be rejoined with their spirits as they come from heaven with Christ and unite in the air (1 Cor. 15:42; 1 Thes. 4:13-18).

Chapter 8

Spiritual Warfare

The need for believers not only to be aware of spiritual warfare but also to be trained to wage it is prevalent throughout the Body of Christ. Those who do not have an elementary understanding of the reality of their spiritual weapons and the enemy we face are ill equipped to live fruitful Christian lives. At the same time, there are some groups that overstate these truths and continually emphasize that God is now building and preparing an army for the end-time battles to come.

This view is problematic in several ways. The truth is, God is not just now building an army. Anyone who has ever been born-again was enlisted immediately from the moment of their spiritual birth to be a soldier in God's army. They were also simultaneously called to be members of His Bride, His Body, His family, and the sheep of His pasture. In addition, they are distinctly His workmanship, created to be participants in His governmental assembly (the Church) whose members serve as ambassadors for the kingdom of God.

All Christians are called to all of this inclusively and to no single function exclusively. When any one of these points is overemphasized, people tend to fade under the weight of the same repetitive analogy. The congregations who excessively stress our membership in the army of God might be refreshed by a furlough wherein they would be reminded of the other functions to which they are called.

1) **Misconception: Most nations are controlled from the heavens by the same spiritual powers that formerly manipulated their ancient civilizations. These aboriginal powers must be deposed before spiritual victory can be achieved in a given geographical region.**

Initially it was the ruling spirit called the prince of Persia who thwarted the heavenly angel's journey to answer Daniel's prayers (Dan. 10:13). However, this same angel told Daniel that the prince of Greece would soon have to be reckoned with as he would replace the present prince of Persia (Dan. 10:20). These verses were referring to the Grecian armies of Alexander the Great who occupied Babylon subsequent to the Persian rule. Apparently, there is a changing of the guard with spiritual powers just as there is with earthly administrations. The contemporary themes of sinful behavior endemic to a region reflect the identities of the spirits of darkness that are motivating them. Therefore, when seeking to identify the rulers in the spiritual realm, it may be wise to consider present day issues rather than the sins of ancient cultures. If spiritual warfare against supposed aboriginal spirits over a region proves ineffective, it is likely that the spiritual diagnosis has been amiss.

2) **Misconception: The rite of exorcism has been performed on my behalf scores of times because I was possessed by hundreds of demons. It was a long process as those who ministered to me thoroughly interrogated the demonic entities that spoke through me to get precise information about Satan's plans against me.**

The ministry of exorcism or deliverance from evil spirits has strong biblical precedents. Any ministry that hopes to duplicate the results of the New Testament's pattern of effective evangelism should embrace it. Jesus, His apostles, and the believers in the early church employed this ministry. They performed exorcisms in the synagogues, hillsides, and streets of the ancient world. Deliverance from evil spirits is not an archaic procedure that can adequately be replaced by modern psychological counseling. Many of the psychological terms used to define disorders are taken from the Greek language. The writers of the New Testament would have been inspired to pen the words "neurosis" and "psychosis" if that is what their subjects had. They cast demons out of people because that is precisely what was needed to be done. Over the past two millennia, technology has advanced, but the basic needs of human nature have not. Some people then and some individuals now need the ministry of exorcism.

The technique that is described at the beginning of this section is a bizarre complication of genuine biblical deliverance. It exaggerates the number of demons that people will normally have, the reliability of demons to tell the truth, and the length of time that it takes to see a person set free. When Jesus and the ministers of the Church performed exorcisms, the process was quick and final. They had the faith to believe that, as they issued anointed authoritative commands, the finger of God would honor their request and extract all demonic influences (Luke 11:20; 10:19). There is no evidence that they routinely interrogated demons in efforts to obtain truthful information (Mark 1:34). Apparently their discernment was sufficient to help them understand that demons are the delegates of the father of lies (John 8:44). They were not interested in giving them opportunities to pollute minds with what the Bible calls the doctrines of demons (1 Tim. 4:1). Most of the time when deliverance was ministered, people were freed from one rather than multiple demons. This was the case with the deaf and mute boy, the woman with a spirit of infirmity, and the man who disturbed the service when Jesus was speaking in the synagogue (Luke 13:10-13; Mark 1:23-26; 9:17-27). In another instance, Paul cast a single demon out of the fortune-telling girl of Philippi (Acts 16:16-19). Certainly all of these people suffered through various devastating traumas during their lives due to the stigma of their afflictions. If this is taken into consideration, it could be concluded that if multiple demonic infestations were common, it would have been apparent in their situations. Normally in written communication, when a number is mentioned it is done so to emphasize something specific or unusual. This was the case with Mary Magdalene as Jesus cast seven demons out of her (Luke 8:1-2). He delivered the Gerasene demoniac of thousands of evil spirits (Mark 5:1-21). However, it must be noted that before his deliverance he was incapable of dwelling in civilized society and possessed violent supernatural strength. There are not many people today who are so afflicted.

The church needs to embrace the ministry of exorcism as there are many who will never know true freedom without it. We should also endeavor to minister it in a biblical manner in order not to complicate the process in a way that will rob them of experiencing the simplicity that is in Christ (2 Cor. 11:3).

3) **Misconception: Thousands of people are the victims of satanic ritual abuse (SRA). When a person comes for deliverance, their repressed memories and family's generational history should be thoroughly examined to make sure that they are not SRA victims. It is not unusual for it to take years to free a person from the consequences of ritual abuse.**

These assumptions likely represent one of Satan's most clever ploys. The Word of God admonishes us not to be naive about his schemes (Eph. 6:11; 2 Cor. 2:11). Now that the reality for the need of exorcism is being restored to the Church, Satan is seeking to complicate the ministry by exaggerating the extent of his influence. Hundreds of people are currently claiming that they have bizarre family histories that have been filled with incidences of occult ritual abuse. The problem is that the majority of these individuals do not have objective proof to validate their claims. For the most part, they state that either they have received subjective revelations of abuse from repressed memories or that it was established as a fact through the spiritual discernment of a counselor. An elementary understanding of the power of suggestion and the deceptiveness of the human heart make these claims highly suspect (Jer. 17:9). The Bible depicts the imagination as a major stronghold of Satan (2 Cor. 10:3-5). He delights in giving people thoughts that exalt his power to hold captives beyond the Cross's power to instantly liberate them (1 Cor. 1:18). It was his rebellious drive to become the center of attention that initially caused him to lose his position as the archangel Lucifer (Isa. 14:12-14). His self-centeredness reduced him to becoming Satan, the archenemy of God.

Today in our society, there is a false assertion that multitudes of people in every level of business and civil authority covertly torture people and sacrifice thousands of infants in satanic worship. This lie comes from the devil's all-consuming desire to be the center of attention. The essential item—objective proof—that would validate these claims is sorely lacking. When one considers the relentless investigative abilities of the secular media to plumb for sensational stories, there is a curious absence of news reports relating occult abuse. Of course, undoubtedly there are isolated incidences of it occurring. But if it were a major problem, we would probably see reports of it regularly on the evening news.

In addition, there is a legitimate need in every person to possess the understanding that they are uniquely distinctive. Those who (falsely or truthfully) regularly remind others that they are SRA victims could be exhibiting a perversion of this cry of the human heart. The only satisfying answer for this cry is the assurance that one was eternally chosen to be a uniquely gifted, adopted child of the living God.

Ritual abuse, however, is not an uncommon factor in ancient civilizations and contemporary heathen cultures in third world nations. In biblical times, the societies of Rome, Greece, and Asia Minor were steeped in aberrant ritualism. Historical records document that the temple of Diana in Ephesus employed 1,500 ritual prostitutes of both sexes. In Greece, Diana was portrayed as the protector of women. Little boys were flogged at her altar yearly to revenge the sins of men against women. The churches that Paul established in both locations grew to mega proportions. Undoubtedly there were hundreds of persons converted who had been subjected to occult abuse. If these acts had the power to mark individuals with devastating wounds that required arduous ministry to heal, Paul would have mentioned it in his writings. His letters offer no specifics about any supposed traumatic results of these customs. To those who had been involved in activities that were included in ritual perversions, he simply said: "And such were some of you. But you were washed, but you were sanctified, but you were justified in the name of the Lord Jesus and by the Spirit of our God" (1 Cor. 6:9-11).

Today there are thousands of people coming to the Lord in third world nations. Many of them do bear the marks of ritual abuse. There are those from African tribes who had their faces cut with designs to protect them from demons when they reached the age of puberty. Many from the Amazon area had their lips and ears stretched to enhance their beauty. Some from India have permanent welts on their backs from self-inflicted fetish floggings. But these who have found Christ simply smile through their scars with a radiance that reflects freedom in Christ and the joy of the Lord. I have been listening to missionary reports for over 50 years. To date, I have yet to hear one report of exhaustive ministry to liberate converts who had been subjected to ritual abuse. It is curious to ponder why third-world converts with ritual abuse histories don't need in-depth ministry, but those from privileged nations do. It is possible that, though we are rich, we are cultivating a spiritual atmosphere that is poor in faith. We have a form of godliness, but we are inclined to underestimate the initial rush of power that comes at salvation to liberate people from life's hurts and transform lives (2 Tim. 3:5-7). Even if these reports of widespread SRA wounds were factual, they could not commonly withstand salvation's instantaneous healing power.

4) **Misconception: I was really hurt by a friend's outburst of anger, but I know it wasn't him. It was just the enemy because we do not wrestle against flesh and blood.**

This position rests on assumptions that are faulty in several ways. The phrase "we wrestle not against flesh and blood" is not offered in relation to our stress points in interpersonal relationships. The context of this wrestling is our spiritual warfare against spirits of evil in the heavenly regions (Eph. 6:12). Secondly, we have the legitimate recourse of rebuking those with whom we have close relationships when they offend us through unbecoming behavior. Most loved ones would attempt to act more charitably if they were allowed the process of being gently scolded for, repenting of, and subsequently forgiven for their offenses (Luke 17:3-4; Gal. 2:11-14).

Finally, this position implies that the singular reason for people's misbehavior is satanic manipulation. The full implications are that if it were not for the enemy, people would inevitably behave properly. Basic Christian doctrine teaches that the primary cause of sin is the active residue of the fallen sinful nature that resides within us. It is described in the Bible as the old man, the body of sin, the law of sin, and the works of the flesh (Rom. 6:6; 7:23; Gal. 5:19-21). Galatians 5 describes actions such as contentiousness and outbursts of anger as *works of the flesh*. The majority of people who are argumentative and explosive in temper have a natural propensity to react in that manner. Demonic influences can intensify and exaggerate human weaknesses, but it cannot create them. When satanic activity from the heavenly regions is a factor, the spiritual warfare of forgiving friends and relatives can quench its intensity (Eph. 6:12). But, nonetheless, every individual remains responsible for his actions. If this were not so, it would be unjust of God to call us into account for the works we have done in the flesh when we stand before His eternal judgement seat (2 Cor. 5:10). The remedy is for every individual to take personal responsibility to reckon themselves dead to sin and alive to righteousness by putting off the old man (Rom. 6:6,11; Eph. 4:21-24).

Chapter 9

Adversities And Temptations

It is not uncommon for Christians to become painfully aware that they are guilty of falling into sin from a temptation. On these occasions, I believe that it is encouraging for us to muse on the court of heaven. Jury tampering has occurred on our behalf. It is as though an angel with high connections has gotten to the Judge and jury and the "fix" is in.

The sheriff of guilt has apprehended you while you were committing a crime. The clarity of your guilt causes the prosecutor, better known as Satan, the accuser of the brethren, to call for your arraignment before the court (Rev. 12:10). You cannot afford a lawyer, so the court secures one for you. The Judge, God the Father, selects His Son who happens to be a lawyer (Psa. 75:7; Heb. 12:3; 1 Jn. 2:1). He is unique because He has never lost a case. Your Advocate chooses a jury of your peers. These are saints who have previously been tried for the misdemeanor with which you are charged. The court is in session, and the Judge opens the trial by reminding the jury that they are to judge others with the equity with which they would want to be judged (Matt. 7:1; Ja. 5:9). The prosecutor points his finger at you and recites his eyewitness account of your crime. Your Advocate majestically rises in your defense. He confidently smiles at the Judge and winks at the jury. He requests that the court dismiss the charges. He explains that you were formerly tried for the same crime and that Another had paid your debt in full (1 Cor. 5:21). He then asks the Judge to search the records to ascertain whether or not there is accurate data for the current charge. The Judge fumbles through His papers and responds that He cannot find any record of the charge. He then smiles and recollects that the charges were forgiven 2,000 years ago and that the record must have been lost in a cloud of paperwork (Isa. 43:25; 44:22). Your Advocate then demands that the case be dropped on the basis of insufficient evidence and double jeopardy. The prosecutor begins to complain about jury tampering on the basis of the Judge's relationship with the defense attorney and the jury's history. The Judge's gavel sounds with finality. Your case is dismissed, and the prosecutor is charged with contempt of court. Take heart. The "fix" is in.

1) Superstition: The presence of adversity indicates the absence of God. If I am in the will of God, things will go smoothly.

If this were true, Paul found the will of God illusive. Rioting hordes stoned him and left him for dead (Acts 14:19). Hostile civil authorities often scourged and incarcerated him for preaching the lordship of Jesus (2 Cor. 11:23-25). Yet, he asserted that those who were faithful in prayer could experience the peace of God that defies human understanding in any circumstance (Phil. 4:6-7). Faithfulness to the will of God will eventually provide a superior level of harmony in most of our endeavors. However, it is doubtful that life will ever be so tranquil that we do not anxiously welcome the righteous rule of the Second Advent of Jesus.

2) **Misconception: Your inability to apprehend blessings indicates that there is hidden sin in your life.**

At times this is true. But it is not the probable cause of most believers' failure to apprehend covenant benefits. God is not a child abuser who punishes His children without first communicating clear and specific warnings before withholding His blessings. Generally speaking, it is innate religious condemnation that keeps us from having the confidence to ask for His blessing in faith. When we are encouraged to believe that He is greater than the condemnation in our hearts, it generates faith to receive the provisions of His grace (1 Jn. 3:20-22). God's first line response to people who are unthankful or even doing evil is kindness (Lk. 6:35). Sin is not always used as a technicality to withhold blessings, but His goodness is regularly employed to bring us to repentance from sin (Rom. 2:4).

3) **Misconception: If I truly loved the Lord and really had faith, I would not repeatedly be tempted to commit my besetting sins.**

Those who embrace this idea mistakenly interpret the sensation of temptation for sin itself. Sin does not occur unless a person follows through and acts upon the temptation. The feeling of being tempted is actually an evidence of God's grace as it serves as a mechanism to alert us to the *potential* for committing sin. When temptation strikes, we need not be discouraged and feel that through its presence we are already sinning and are obligated to complete the process. We have the option of denying the temptation the opportunity to escalate into full-blown sin.

Perhaps one of the most common areas in which we feel temptation is in the realm of sexual lusts. It is encouraging to understand that we are not alone in this temptation. Every person who has ever lived, including the Lord Jesus, has been confronted with this issue. That's right, even the Lord was tempted with spontaneous, uninvited sexual thoughts! Here on earth, He did not breeze through on His Deity. He lived life as a man who was tempted like we are but was unique in that He never let the temptations bloom into sins. Surely, He was God, but He was also fully a man. He was equipped with the same hormone levels and the same risk of possible temptation which all healthy men experience. That is why He can empathize with the feelings of our temptations because He, too, experienced them (Heb. 4:15).

4) **Superstition: I cannot prosper due to the negative words that others are speaking against me.**

There is a reality to the power of negative speech, particularly when uttered by a person who has God-given authority in a person's life. A parent, a spouse, or a spiritual leader could potentially wield a sufficient level of authority to invoke a curse. A primary benefit of salvation is that it reverses all curses (Gal. 3:13-14). When a curse is recognized in a believer's life, it can easily be revoked by a singular confession of repentance, forgiveness, and freedom concerning it. In relation to negative speech from individuals who do not have authority in our lives, we might all do well to be challenged by the example of politicians. Many of them are subjected to daily bombardments of scurrilous accusations from saints and sinners alike. Nonetheless, term after term, they seek re-election and enjoy above average productivity throughout their lives.

5) **Misconception: Job had his trials, and Paul was given a thorn in the flesh. Therefore, we can anticipate that God will use affliction to chasten us.**

Yes, Job certainly had trouble, and Paul certainly had some type of thorn in the flesh, but few people meet their qualifications. Job was more righteous than anyone on earth during his day and was extremely wealthy (Job 1:1-3,8). He was so revered for his wisdom and generosity that old men would stop talking and young men would stand to their feet when he came on the scene (Job 29:8-9). In addition, most commentaries state that he received back twice his former wealth and was physically healed within nine months of his affliction.

Paul was given a thorn to keep him from becoming arrogant because of his abundant revelations. He did seek the Lord on three occasions, asking for deliverance from his affliction. This seeking to alleviate his suffering clearly indicates that Paul understood that God normally delivers His people from troubles. The Lord's response was that His grace would be sufficient for him in the midst of the affliction (2 Cor. 12:7-9). When a person is truly given grace for a hardship, they can live with it in a totally victorious and productive manner. To those who observe them, their condition may seem unbearable. But the truth is, the afflicted person is not in the least bit thwarted by it because it does not hinder their fruitfulness or peace one iota.

Few people meet either Job's or Paul's qualifications! Unlike Job, they have never been quite that outstanding in their righteousness, reputation, or accomplishments. Unlike Paul, they are not so saturated with continual meaningful revelations from on High that they are at risk of becoming obnoxious with pride.

When it comes to chastening, there are some reasonable questions to ask: "Weren't you warned, and why have you not repented of such gross misbehavior that would warrant severe punishment?" "How has this affliction increased your pursuit of holiness?" (Heb. 12:9-10). God is not a child abuser. He is a better Father than our earthly fathers who disciplined us. He would never punish us without ample warning. In the rare instances where God is using physical affliction as a tool of chastening, it is never His will that it be perpetual. The punishment will end when the person repents of his misbehavior and turns to God for healing.

6) **Misconception: End-time persecution will bring unity to the Church.**

Personal experience and the words of Jesus do not support this viewpoint. For many years I worked among the persecuted churches in the former Soviet block of Eastern Europe. My observation was that the Lord's prediction of the last days was accurate when He said that brothers would betray one another as their agape love waned under the weight of persecution (Matt. 24:9-14). I sadly saw a shocking degree of jealousy, suspicion, and disunity between churches.

On the other hand, the greatest unifier I have observed is among churches of all denominations that have embraced the current move of the Spirit known as the Renewal or the Father's Blessing. A major fountainhead for this movement has been the Toronto Airport Christian Fellowship in Canada. We might all do well to pray that the Lord would hold off persecution and send visitations of the Holy Spirit to fall on every church.

Chapter 10

Faith to Apprehend God's Blessings

There is an athletic term that is used of a player when they have performed to the optimum of their ability. When complimented, they often respond: "I was in the zone." There is also a "zone" in which a believer can function in relation to their individual faith to apprehend various forms of material blessings from God. When this happens, the faith projects that once took arduous efforts of prayer begin to flow in unprecedented abundance. Those who operate in this "faith zone" find that before they call, God hears them, and while they are still speaking He answers their requests (Isa. 65:24 LB).

It takes time for a Christian to cultivate their faith to a sufficient level that would enable them to abide in the zone of abundance for life's daily provisions. The process is similar to the maturing process of babies from infancy to the pre-school stage. One of the things that can cause babies to cry is that they are hungry. They fret because they are unsure about whether or not they will be fed. At a certain point in their growth process, something "clicks" in their minds, and they no longer cry for food. They have passed into a zone where they have full confidence that mother will feed them, even if she, at times, happens to be a little off schedule. Jesus admonished His disciples that they were not to fret about their daily provisions (Matt. 6:31-33). Certainly no one mature enough to become part of the Lord's apostolic team should have been concerned over such matters. However, we all must be baby saints before we can become mature disciples. During this period, it is healthy to spend time praying about material matters. Time will pass, and we will see that God never fails to deliver our daily provision in response to our prayers of faith. Then one day, "click" it happens. We pass into the faith zone. From that day on, we will not have to pray so continuously about our needs because it will be settled in our spirits that they are already met. Instead, we will walk in a spirit of thankfulness for our daily provision.

1) **Misconception: Every Christian has been given the same measure of faith. If you need any provision of the New Covenant, you can rely on your original measure of faith.**

The Bible and Christian experience do not vindicate this doctrine. It is built upon the King James Version of Romans 12:3 where it says, "God hath dealt to every man the measure of faith." Verse six of this same passage does not support this theory as it reads, "Having then gifts differing according to the grace that is given to us, whether prophecy, let us prophesy according to the proportion of faith." The implication is that each believer is given grace for different gifts. We are to minister those gifts in accordance with the proportion of our level of faith in that gift. The Scriptures describe Jesus as having been given the Holy Spirit without measure (John 3:34). Jesus admonished His apostles on several occasions for having little faith (Matt. 8:26). They, in turn, requested that He increase their faith (Luke 17:5). These factors indicate that faith is a spiritual commodity that is administered in different levels, and it can be increased.

In addition, there is the *gift of faith*. The spontaneous impartation of this gift can temporarily empower a person with a level of faith for a specific task that exceeds their normal faith capacity. It is not unusual for the Lord to increase our faith in new areas through the gift of faith (1 Cor. 12:5-11). At times, our gift of faith for today for a certain task can be our level of increased faith for the same task tomorrow.

The idea that all have the same measure of faith can readily be observed as a misconception in Christian experience. Most every pastor has a burden for the lost. Few have the faith necessary to fill stadiums and heal the sick as do gifted evangelists.

2) **Misconception: If you want to appropriate a particular form of God's blessings, all you need do is confess the verses related to it and you will have it.**

In Proverbs 25:2 it says: "It is the glory of God to conceal a matter, but the glory of kings is to search out a matter." God desires fellowship with us, and one of the best ways for Him to insure that we stay in constant fellowship with Him is that our apprehension of particular blessings can never be reduced to a set formula. The potential for His blessings for us as "kings" is a constant, but He varies the approach that we use to apprehend a particular form of blessing. One time when we desire a certain blessing, all we need do is quote this verse and that verse and since $2 + 2 = 4$ (e.g., reading a verse plus prayer = healing), and we receive the provision that we needed. But, the next time it does not work simply because He wants us to *seek Him* for a new approach for that particular blessing. This time the equation may be $1 + 1 + 2 = 4$ (e.g., an adjustment in attitude and diet plus prayer from two friends to receive the desired blessing).

3) **Misconception: Job's calamities were due to his fear and lack of faith.**

Sincere saints, who feel obligated to embellish the dealings of God, propagate this doctrine. They present Him with humanistic understandings of goodness that exempt Him from all responsibility for the hardships that His people endure. The reality is that God is good *all of the time,* and He does not need our help in the presentation of His character. Both the Old and New Testaments reveal that God was the initiator of Job's trials and had benevolent purposes in doing so (Ja. 5:11). God unashamedly took full responsibility for Job's situation (Job 2:3-6). Apparently He accepted Satan's challenge to test Job as a proof that His man would remain faithful to Him. Job did confess that what he had feared had come upon him (Job 3:25). The form of fear that he had was a legitimate reverential caution. If it was not a reasonable fear, God would not have labeled him as blameless in all of his ways because carnal fearfulness is a weakness that God will not tolerate (Job 1:8; Rev. 21:8). Job was not lacking in faith because he is described as one who was unique in uprightness in comparison to those living in his generation (Job 1:1,8). If God notes that a person's uprightness has pleased Him, it stands to reason that they have faith because without faith it is impossible to please God (Heb. 11:6).

4) **Misconception: It is wrong to use our faith to apprehend material blessings. Faith should be used for spiritual pursuits such as the salvation of lost souls.**

Seeking God for tangible blessings is a point of stumbling for many Christians whose thinking has been blurred by the limitations of the traditional teachings of the Church. Tradition has limited the expectations of our faith merely to spiritual blessings such as inner peace, revelation from passages of Scripture, and seeing one's church grow and loved ones evangelized. Certainly, these matters are primary. But they by no means exhaust the extent of the biblical blessings of God. To the contrary, when blessings are mentioned in the Word of God, more often than not, it is in relation to the acquisition of success, wealth, and health, rather than overtly spiritual matters. For example, in 3 John 2, the Apostle John describes how he prayed for his constituents: "Beloved, I pray that you may prosper in all things and be in health, just as your soul prospers." When John was praying for the churches under his care, it was his wish and intercession that they would enjoy prosperity and physical health to the same measure at which they were progressing spiritually in their souls.

In the Lord's Prayer, Jesus said that we should regularly pray for our daily bread and deliverance from evil. Getting daily bread throughout a lifetime implies the need for education, vocational training, transportation, suitable clothing, and some form of savings for retirement years. To secure these things, one must be blessed with physical health and reasonable financial success. The word for "evil" that's used in the Lord's Prayer comes from a Greek root that means "labor which does not stop short of demanding the whole strength of a man." This definition implies that it is not God's will for any of us to continually work so many hours that we do not have the physical or mental strength to enjoy life. To live free from this kind of labor takes money.

The following are some other scriptures which clearly reveal that blessings primarily pertain to tangible things and physical health: Gen. 24:35; Deut. 28:2-13; Psa. 112:1-3; Prov. 10:22; Ex. 23:25.

5) **Misconception: It is improper for Christians to have the ambition to get ahead in life and be successful.**

This is far from the picture that God presents in His Word

of the legitimate desires of human nature and the ambitions of His choicest servants. The ambition to be successful resides in the breast of every man. Practically everyone has an inner drive to advance either in income or title. We all enjoy recognition from our peers when we have achieved something of note. The lordship of Jesus over our lives does not nullify this drive. To the contrary, it intensifies it. All who embrace the cross of Christ are equipped to become high achievers. To achieve success, we have the Word to instruct us, the Holy Spirit to guide us, and the testimony of God's champions to inspire us.

King David and the Apostle Peter were both men who were deeply committed to the purposes of God. Though both were willing to sacrifice all for God, they were still compelled by their desires for rewards. They understood that it was legal for spiritually minded people to have the ambition to advance in life in order to bless their families financially. The Lord did not upbraid them for their ambition; He subtly used it as a motivating factor in getting His purposes accomplished.

David's initial motivation for killing the giant was neither religious nor ethnic pride. His first desire was to win the King's bounty (1 Sam. 17:24-32). David had overheard the soldiers when they commented that anyone who killed Goliath would be rewarded with: marriage to the king's daughter (hopefully the pretty one), great riches, and tax exemption for his entire family. He asked the men to repeat themselves three different times; he wanted to make sure that he had heard correctly. Once he had grasped the reality of the reward, he would not be denied. He pushed through his brothers' criticism and King Saul's apprehensions. He boldly announced, "Sir, your problems are over. I'll put this guy down."

Peter reminded Jesus that he and the other apostles had given up everything for Him saying, "See, we have left all and followed You." So Jesus answered and said, "Assuredly, I say to you, there is no one who has left house or brothers or sisters or father or mother or wife or children or lands, for My sake and the Gospel's, who shall not receive a hundredfold now in this time—houses and brothers and sisters and mothers and children and lands, with persecutions—and in the age to come, eternal life (Mark 10:28-30).

Note that the Lord did not rebuke him for the sins of ruthless self-ambition or the love of money. The Master did not patronize Peter with some religious cliché about rewards in the by-and-by. He knew how to get the best out of His employee— He assured him that all who sacrificed on behalf of the kingdom would receive 100 fold (10,000%) reward in this life, plus eternal life in the future.

It must be noted that the Lord added that persecution would come with the rewards. The persecution arises on two fronts. The first comes from Satan, who will make every effort to keep Christians swimming in the sea of obscurity; and secondly, from uninformed believers who equate piety with poverty and humility with aimless mediocrity.

6) Misconception: I am a Christian, and I have always struggled financially. Jesus said that the poor would always be with us and that we are to deny ourselves. I guess it is simply my plight to be poor.

Jesus said that the poor would always be among us, but He did not say that the same people would continually be poor (Matt. 26:11). To the contrary, we are to advance from faith to faith and use our faith to provide for our families. Using one's faith to provide adequately for one's family is a major tenant of biblical Christianity. Romans 1:17 says, "For in it the righteousness of God is revealed from faith to faith; as it is written, 'The just shall live by faith.'" 1 Tim. 5:8 says, "But if anyone does not provide for his own, and especially for those of his household, he has denied the faith and is worse than an unbeliever."

Jesus did instruct those who wished to follow Him to deny themselves by taking up their cross daily (Luke 9:23). A person's struggle with financial insufficiency does not qualify as their cross simply because they can neither embrace it nor ignore it at will. In reality, one cannot deny themselves of anything that is not truly within their grasp. If you earn $100,000 per year and choose to live on $20,000 in order to give the balance to missions, you are denying yourself. If you settle for a poverty line income when others, no more gifted than you, are earning more, you are not denying yourself—you are simply unwise.

7) Misconception: Well, money can't buy love or health.

Any sensible person knows that this is true. Any thinking person is also aware that though money cannot buy love or health, it is certainly an answer to many of the problems that frustrate love and hinder good health. This fact is supported in the Scriptures by a verse which shocks religious minds, Eccles. 10:19: "A feast is made for laughter, And wine makes merry; But money answers everything." Money is often the Lord's delegated means to alleviate the stress in love relationships that are waning because of continual financial hardships. He does give us money to provide transportation to the healing evangelist's meeting. He does give us incomes which can afford health plans to better insure our ongoing health.

8) Misconception: Divine healing is always God's will.

God has never withdrawn the power gifts of faith, healing, and miracles from the Church. Jesus is the same yesterday, today, and forever (Heb. 13:8). Through His Body, the Church, He is still walking about, doing good, and healing all forms of the devil's oppression (Acts 10:38). Christians from denominational backgrounds that have historically rejected divine healing are now discovering that it is a powerful tool of evangelism. Evangelical and charismatic churches around the world are holding healing services. The fellowships that obey the injunctions of the Scriptures by anointing the sick with oil are witnessing rewarding numbers of miracles in answer to their prayers of faith (Ja. 5:13-16).

On the other side of the coin, nearly every church that believes in healing has been confronted with disappointing situations that belie the statement that it is always God's will to heal. Most of us know of dear saints who were exemplary in their faith and ran the full gamut of spiritual exercises in their efforts to be healed. They were anointed with oil, renounced curses, had demons of infirmity bound, sought the physicians, made endless visits to the healing evangelists, and made a positive confession that they were healed, but yet they did not experience healing. These dear ones were not condemned to death because they were negligent in some technical application of their faith. God is sovereign, and He works all things after the counsel of His will (Eph. 1:11). If He willed for them to be healed, any of the aforementioned techniques of faith could have been sufficiently anointed to bring forth their healing. God does not take lightly the death of His saints (Psa. 116:15). He values the timing of their deaths according to His predetermined plan for their life spans. Outside of those who are alive at the coming of the Lord, all men have a divine appointment with death and judgment (Heb. 9:27). None will be late for these appointments, and no disease or human failure can facilitate an untimely demise.

Chapter 11

Devotional Life

It was our twenty-fifth wedding anniversary. Prudence and I had scheduled a lovely evening at a posh restaurant. We slept in late and then headed off in our respective cars to the hairdresser and barber. I was driving a new Nissan pick-up that had been given to me by a member of another church.

Suddenly my bubble of contentment was burst by an all too familiar inner voice. The voice of condemnation began to taunt me. "Here you are driving along in a beautiful truck that God graciously gave you. You have a wonderful wife who has borne with you through your numerous shenanigans for all these long years. It is nearly noon on a day that most would praise God for, and you have not offered a single word of prayer or praise. You're an ingrate that by no means deserves the quality of life that God has so bountifully showered upon you."

Of course I listened, and as was my custom began to slip into the repentance mode of a miserable offender. Just as I was determining where to pull off the road to read my Bible and worship, I heard another voice; actually it was a sigh of frustration that audibly filled the cab of my truck. Within that sigh there was an underlying message that came to me by revelation.

It was as though the sigh indicated, "Oh, no. Not this song and dance again. If you are bent on praising God, you can do it while you're driving. You don't have to pull off of the road in order for Him to be convinced of your sincerity." The revelation continued within me. It dawned on me that I, along with many other saints, was the prisoner of religious guilt in relation to my devotional life. It seemed that I was never quite able to appease the negative inner voice. If I was reading my Bible, it goaded me to sing worship choruses. If I was singing, it insisted that I would be more pleasing to God if I prostrated myself in silence before Him. A kind voice now sounded from within the truck, "Free God's people from guilt." I believe that the voice I heard was that of an angel. Since that day it has been my joy to follow his injunction.

1) **Misconception: The only member of the Godhead that should be directly addressed during prayer is the Father.**

This philosophy is built upon Jesus' instructions about praying what is commonly called the Lord's Prayer and prayers for provision (Matt. 6:6-15; John 16:23). It is orthodox to address our prayers to the Father as we pray in the authority of Jesus' name. However, the Bible indicates that the members of the first century church were not limited to this form of communication as they communed with God. They understood that through salvation they were invited into fellowship with the Father, the Son, and the Holy Spirit (Philip. 2:1; 1 John 1:3). The Greek word for "fellowship" indicates the intimate sharing of life that includes communication. Jesus promised the disciples that He would not leave them as orphans because the Holy Spirit would be sent to abide with them. When Jesus was on earth, He was the constant companion of His disciples. He talked with them and answered their questions. It is His intention that we each have the same caliber of companionship that would necessitate two-way communication with the Holy Spirit as a person. If we are living with anything less, we are existing needlessly as spiritual orphans.

Jesus said that we are to pray that the Lord of the harvest will send forth laborers (Matt. 9:38). The Holy Spirit was acting in His role as the Lord of the harvest in Acts 13:2 when He said, "Now separate to Me, Barnabas and Saul for the work to which I have called them." The Apostle Paul and Barnabas had verbal interchanges with the resurrected Lord (Acts 9:5,10; 18:9-10). When the deacon, Stephen, was being stoned to death, he prayed directly to Jesus (Acts 7:59-60). If it is wrong to pray to Jesus, Stephen picked an inappropriate moment to depart into heresy.

2) **Superstition: In order for a prayer to be effectual, it must conclude with the words: "In Jesus' Name, amen."**

It is legitimate to end prayers with the name of Jesus, but it is by no means a mandate in order for one's prayers to be effective. The tradition that asserts that prayers must end in that manner has evolved through our contemporary misunderstanding of the biblical meaning of phrases such as "in the name of Jesus" and "in My name" (Mk. 16:17; Jn. 16:22-24; Eph. 5:20; Col. 3:17). When this phraseology is used in the Scriptures, it primarily denotes the authority that we have as we pray, rather than the mandatory ending for our prayers. The wording "in the name of" is synonymous with "in the authority of." An example of this is found in Acts 3:1-8 when the apostle Peter gave the command for the cripple to rise up and walk in the name of Jesus of Nazareth (Acts 16:18). Christ's legacy to His Church is that He has delegated to us the same power the Father endowed Him with for His victorious resurrection (Matt. 28:18-19; Jn. 20:21).

We can pray with the faith that our prayers are heard if we

carry the inner conviction that we are operating as delegates of Jesus Christ. We are ambassadors for Christ (2 Cor. 5:20) and can be compared to ambassadors who represent their nations on foreign soil. Just as they conduct their business with the confidence that they are backed by their respective governments, so too can we pray and minister with the full assurance that we are backed with the authority of the kingdom of God. There are occasions where we might demonstrate more faith in Jesus by simply laying hands on people to impart blessing and healing than we would by specifically ending the prayers with "In Jesus' name, amen" (Mark 6:5; 10:16; Acts 8:17-19).

3) Superstition: The devil jumped me because I forgot to put on my spiritual armor before leaving for work this morning.

The action of verbally putting on one's spiritual armor can be a helpful reminder that there may be spiritual battles during the day (Eph. 6:11-17). Actually, however, the various parts of this armor are not items that can be put on instantaneously—they are qualities of Christian character and discipline that require time to cultivate. We are not truly girded with truth unless we are committed to being truthful. The Word of God cannot be wielded as a sword unless a person has disciplined himself to memorize it. Any Christian who is unprepared to spontaneously bring the peace of the Gospel into the stresses of daily life is spiritually barefoot. The devil is likely more prone to want to avoid believers who have cultivated the character qualities associated with the armor of God as permanent fixtures in their lives. Those who have not done so are much easier prey.

4) Misconception: A yearly ritual of extended fasting is an advisable practice for those who desire to mature in the Lord.

Fasting is the abstinence from food for spiritual purposes. Jesus implied that His followers would be accustomed to the discipline of fasting (Matt. 6:16-17). Congregations and individuals who are led by the Spirit to occasionally set themselves apart for periods of combined fasting and prayer can reap wonderful benefits. It has the potential to increase spiritual sensitivity and to obliterate stubborn sin and health issues (Isa. 58:6-12). The problem is that some dear saints tend to think that more frequent and longer fasts are better fasts. The two biblical synonyms for fasting, "humbling" and "chastening," reveal indications about the nature of fasting (Psa. 35:13; 69:10). The two implications are that when a person fasts they should do so in humility, and they will likely experience elements of physical discomfort due to their self-imposed, sacrificial chastening. Those who fast so frequently that they feel neither humble nor chastened are at risk of quenching the effectiveness of their abstinence. Unless one is anointed to do so, habitual fasting might better qualify as poor eating habits or vain attempts at weight control cloaked in sanctimonious trappings. The definitive question for all fasts, and particularly long ones, should be: Are we led by the Spirit? The Bible provides only four incidents in which heroes of the faith embarked on 40-day fasts. The men involved were Moses, Elijah, and Jesus. In each of these incidents, the fasting was prompted by the direct leading of the Spirit and the voice of God (Ex. 24:16-18; Deut. 9:9,18; 1 Kings 19:7-8; Matt. 4:1-2). In addition, each of these participants withdrew themselves from all secular activities for the duration of their fasts.

5) Superstition: I have not read my Bible for several days, and I really feel that I have failed the Lord.

Well-meaning ministers of the Gospel unwittingly foster ritualistic legalism by challenging their constituents to emulate their own regimental daily devotions. Their freedom from secular employment enables them to give generous portions of time to formal prayer, reading the Bible, and other devotional pursuits. Their followers sense guilt and tend to condemn themselves when they fail to find the time to follow the regimens that these ministers claim are the evidence of true spirituality. Historically, nations have been reshaped through the faith of people who have not been privileged to read the Bible daily. The members of the first century church did not own Bibles because it was not compiled yet. The majority of them could not have read it even if they possessed one, since they were illiterate. Today, politically oppressed nations like China are aflame with evangelism, yet most of the Christians there have never even seen a complete copy of the Bible. Like the members of the early church, they glean what they can from the meetings that they are able to attend and then meditate on the truths they have heard (1 Thes. 5:27). Their primary point of inspiration is the voice of the Comforter within them (John 14:26). They rest in the joy that, through salvation, they have become the abode of the Father, Son, and Holy Spirit (John 14:21,23). Christians whose formal devotional lives are sporadic need not labor under condemnation. Any believer who endeavors to be sensitive to the inner voice of God, offers spontaneous praises and prayers, and intermittently meditates on scriptural truths throughout the day has found the heart of true spirituality (John 10:3,14; 1 Thes. 5:16-19).

Chapter 12

Matters of Guidance

Without question, one of the primary issues that causes Christians the most anguish is their lack of confidence that they have the ability to ascertain the will of God. Many almost need a burning bush sign before they can believe that they are proceeding in His will. God sometimes does give us overtly spiritual signs for guidance, but that is not the primary way in which He chooses to reveal His will. At salvation He wholly redeems our entire being, including our normal inner cognitive processes. Before salvation, we were under the influence of the prince of the power of the air and routinely obeyed his nudges (Eph. 2:1-3). None of us had to beseech Satan to give us guidance for the day to do his will. We just naturally seemed inclined toward it. God guides the redeemed by using the natural decisions for a day's activities that emerge from within our thought processes. Our guidance is much like driving a car with power steering—it does not work unless the car is moving. As we proceed through our personal decisions for the day, we can depend on God's Spirit to check us if we are going the wrong way (Phil. 2:13). Salvation graduates us to the status of being "naturally supernatural." Most of our guidance from the Holy Spirit is what I call "unconscious guidance." He subtly leads us in a manner that we often do not recognize as divine until after the fact.

For example, I had a month off from work in 1971. I became bored and decided that the best way to spend my time was in prayer. About eight times during that month I made a 30 mile round trip to spend time in intercession with a lady who was a real prayer warrior. This woman had a son who was an unequivocal rebel and disappointment to her, making a mockery of all she treasured. Every time I drove to their house, to my chagrin, she was never home. On the way back, I would browbeat myself for wasting my time.

About a month after I returned to work, my wife called me while I was on the road. She said our friend's son had gotten high on drugs and had come to church to break up the service. She gleefully reported that the Holy Spirit had altered his plan, and he went forward to be born again. Shortly thereafter, he requested a counseling session with me. In our session, he surprisingly revealed: "You know, you are the reason that I am saved." I asked him how that could possibly be. His response was, "Last summer I was thinking about giving my life to the Lord. A number of times I asked God for a sign. I said, 'Lord, if Jim Croft comes to our house today, I will know that You want me.' As soon as I would get the words out of my mouth, you would come driving down our driveway. It frightened me so badly that I would run to the woods and hide." Eight times he was confronted with God reaching out to him with a sign, until the night arrived when he had decided to terrorize the service and found that he could resist God's love no longer. Today that man is one of the leading missionaries in Central America!

1) **Misconception: I'm not going to take another step until I get a prophetic word as confirmation.**

This posture escalates the value of personal prophecy as a primary source of guidance beyond the parameters of the Scriptures and practical wisdom. The New Testament does present prophecy as a legitimate gift of the Holy Spirit that is guardedly encouraged. However, its primary function is to edify, exhort, and comfort congregations with spontaneous utterances that reinforce the precious promises that are clearly revealed in the Bible (1 Cor. 14:3). At times, it can serve as an effective tool of evangelism to alert unbelievers to the reality that God knows their hearts and their deeds (1 Cor. 14:24-25). Prophecy can also be helpful in giving believers insights in relation to their particular spiritual callings (1 Tim. 4:14).

The Scriptures describe prophecy as a desirable gift that is not to be despised (1 Thes. 5:20-21). This implies that there can be something about the nature of the gift that might motivate people to view it as despicable. Most likely this is fostered by the reality that when the gift is used, there is a mixture of divine and human influences present. Any legitimate prophecy will, at best, contain only elements of divine inspiration (1 Cor. 13:9; 14:29). The balance of the utterance will carry varying degrees of the doctrinal views and soulish influences of the person who is offering it. It is these soulish influences that cause the seeking of prophecy for confirmation to be a perilous venture.

The safest ground for confirmation is threefold: It is the reliability of the Scriptures, mature counsel, and the redeemed nature. Salvation gives us the ability to be naturally supernatural. Before conversion, we were all guided by the natural but unsanctified cognitive processes and desires of our souls. We are now guided by sanctified supernatural influences on those same processes from within. Our redeemed minds are trustworthy because God inspires our desires (Philip. 2:13). If one is seeking guidance, prayerfully evaluate what it is that you truly desire to do. Any desire that is biblically ethical and that can be maintained in prayer is most likely correct.

2) Superstition: I'll put a fleece before the Lord. If so and so calls or such and such happens, I will know that I am to do xyz.

The biblical precedents for putting fleeces before the Lord are limited. Gideon is the primary example, and he did it on only two successive occasions to confirm the legitimacy of his calling. Putting out fleeces can degenerate into a forbidden practice called the observing of omens (Deut. 18:10). One who observes omens attempts to acquire prophetic insights through natural events. Believers who overuse fleeces will inevitably begin to get the feeling that they have been fleeced. The observance of omens will eventually produce only perplexing, disappointing fruit. The Word of God, the witness of the Spirit, and the wisdom of mature advisors are to be our primary means of guidance.

3) Superstition: The atmosphere of my secular work environment is so oppressive that I find it impossible to function. I think the Lord wants me to get a job with a Christian firm.

Daniel and his three friends were promoted above their peers in the midst of captivity among heathen soothsayers and astrologers (Dan. 1:11-21). We have a better covenant, established on better promises (Heb. 8:6). Christians should be able to shine as lights regardless of the intensity of the forces of darkness encamped about them.

4) Superstition: Godly or negative spiritual forces orchestrate every minute detail of life.

There are strategic events in all of our lives that are ordered by the Lord (Judges 14:1-4). There are times when the mundane turns out to be significantly blessed or complicated by the corresponding spiritual powers that are motivating it. But, most things in life occur like they do simply because they have the God-ordained potential to do so. If it rains on the day of the church picnic, it does not indict the pastor as being insensitive to the Spirit in his scheduling. If you have a flat tire on the way to the prayer meeting, it does not mean that the devil was personally trying to keep you from going. During the original creation, God put the second law of thermodynamics into play—the law of entropy. Entropy causes the energy that gives form to material things to diminish in its availability over time. It is the major reason that tires go flat—they simply wear out. On the other hand, if four brand new tires go flat in the same week, an emissary of Satan is probably pounding you.

5) Misconception: I believe that our church's dwindling membership has a purpose similar to Gideon's army being cut from 32,000 to 300 warriors.

All who sincerely embrace this posture would be a blessing to their churches if they would pray the analogy through to completion. Gideon's army of volunteers was reduced to 300 *only for the initial attack* on the Midianite camp. Once they were put to flight, all the soldiers who had previously left rejoined the battle and completely subdued the enemy (Judges 7:22-25).

Chapter 13

Sex And Matters of Conscience

The Bible admonishes us to lay aside the sins that so easily beset us (Heb. 12:1). The cessation of committing a particular sin is the ideal form of putting it aside. Some of us find this easier said than done. We are scandalized with ourselves over the actuality that we continually struggle with the same sin. God does not condone a sin that may be ongoing in our lives, but He does have an alternative way of absolving our misery over it. In 2 Timothy 1:12 it says: "For this reason I also suffer these things; nevertheless I am not ashamed, for I know whom I have believed and am persuaded that He is able to keep what I have committed to Him until that Day."

If we have a besetting temptation that has stubbornly resisted every spiritual discipline that we know, we can commit it to the Lord until the day of the final judgment. This means that He takes full responsibility for its presence in our lives. If the temptation knocks and we comply, we simply say, "Lord I ask for your forgiveness because I am sorry. However, I am not ashamed for I have committed this matter to Jesus." Those who do this can depend on the Lord to handle it in one of two possible scenarios. Prior to the Second Coming and our appearance before the judgment seat, He will extract it from our lives. Or, when the issue comes up as we stand before God, He will step forward and say, "Father, the matter is my responsibility because it was committed to me. This person trusted me to either deliver them or take responsibility for it. Father, this was covered at Calvary." I have found that those who employ this strategy often testify that the power of their besetting sin gradually dissipated and then vanished.

1) **Misconception: Since it is a sin to partake of alcoholic beverages, Jesus made grape juice for the wedding at Cana.**

Without question it is a sin to drink to the point of intoxication. However, Christians who want to enjoy alcohol in moderation are not obligated to comply with other's consciences in the matter (Col. 2:16). The conviction that Christians must totally abstain from alcohol is a *cultural* prohibition rather than a *biblical* mandate. Primarily American evangelicals and those of other nations who have been influenced by them perpetuate this view. Many dedicated believers in Germany freely drink beer with no pangs of conscience. I personally know of a Bible school in Portugal where they routinely serve wine with meals. Interestingly, the school is funded by an American denomination that forbids alcohol.

The original language of the Gospels makes it clear that Jesus drank and created intoxicating wine, yet He was without sin. During His earthly ministry, Jesus was criticized for frequenting the haunts of known sinners and accused of being a winebibber (Luke 7:33-34). The criticism would have been pointless if He only drank grape juice. His first miracle was to make 120 gallons of wine for a wedding when the supply had been exhausted (John 2:1-10). If there were 100 guests, His miracle would have potentially made over one gallon available for each of them. The kind of wine they were serving at the feast was the intoxicating type; it was not grape juice. We know this from the word used for wine and the phrase that the master of the feast made when he complimented the bridegroom for the quality of wine that he was serving at the end of the festivities. The official stated that it was customary to serve an inferior wine after the guests had "well drunk" (KJV). This phrase is one word in Greek, and it means to drink to intoxication. If the beverage that was being served was non-alcoholic it would have been senseless for him to use this word. In addition, unlike wine, grape juice is not ranked by quality.

2) **Superstition: God will bless me when He knows that He can trust me with His blessings.**

The fallacy of this is demonstrated through two gifts that we all possess: the ability to speak and to reproduce. If trust were an issue, it would seem that God would be more concerned with the distribution of vocal cords and sexual organs than material blessings. The fact is He has given us all things for our enjoyment regardless of our ability to misuse them (Rom. 8:32; 1 Tim. 6:17).

3) **Misconception: Masturbation is a legitimate form of sexual release for the unmarried. The Bible makes no explicit prohibitions concerning it. Unmarried couples are free to gratify one another sexually as long as they do not engage in genital to genital sex.**

Jesus said that anyone who looked on another person in lust was no less guilty of immorality than one who had actually engaged in an illicit sex act with another individual (Matt. 5:27-28). Seldom, if ever, is one thinking of asexual things when engaging in masturbation. This being true, it is reasonable to assume that the severity of the sin is intensified when one executes a sexual release when fantasizing or from another's stimulation.

4) Misconception: Homosexuals are born with a natural propensity to express themselves sexually with those of the same gender. God would never punish anyone who was faithful to a partner of the same sex throughout his or her life.

The Bible states that homosexuality is an acquired desire. It is contracted when men begin to experiment in sexual practices with other men in ways that differ from the normal sexual union with women (Rom. 1:25-28). Even in the rare instances when a person is born with that desire, they have no more of a legitimate right to express it than they do other prohibited propensities. Some people are born with a weakness for alcohol and others with the potential for murderous rage. Those who continually vent these desires and do not repent will lose their place in the kingdom of God (Gal. 5:19-21). If anyone is born with an intense weakness for a specific sin, God requires that they quench it. It is not life threatening to do so. One can go to heaven with unfulfilled sinful desires. No one can see God unless they have denied their unlawful passions in the active pursuit of holiness (Col. 3:5; Heb. 12:14).

Chapter 14

Outreach to the Backslidden
And the Lost

I am convinced that many of the people whom we refer to as "backsliders" really do not fit the definition. They may have stopped attending Christian gatherings, but they have not quit relating to God. I have talked with a number of such people and they express that they still love the Lord and consider their faith of preeminent importance in their lives. The problem is they simply cannot cope with the hyper-religiosity of some of the Lord's people. They found it overwhelming to continually attempt to meet church people's expectations on how they should spend their time and energies. Coming back to God is not the issue; they just do not want to come back to us.

A fellow minister cited an interesting statistic that was taken from a survey conducted among individuals living in Los Angeles, California. Seventy percent of those who professed faith in Jesus and the born-again salvation experience reported that they no longer attended a church of any type although most, at one time, had been members of congregations. It is probable that this is an indication that there is something in the religious atmosphere of those fellowships that drove them away. It certainly was not a lack of choice when it comes to denominational variety. California has been a hot spot for creative innovations in that department. If you cannot find it in L. A., it is doubtful that it is available anywhere. It could be that the answer lies in some of the factors that I touched upon in the preface to this book. If this is true, we need to ask the Lord to send us a refreshing that will make us more appealing to those who no longer attend church as well as to the lost (Acts 3:19-21). It could be that the Lord could refrain from giving us a great ingathering until we have taken away the rubbish that prevents people from being comfortable around us (Neh. 4:10).

1) Misconception: To become a member of the family of God you must be able to recall a specific occasion in which you personally asked Jesus to come into your heart and be your Lord and Savior. Anyone who has never done so is going to hell.

This view is amiss in that it restricts one's understanding of those who qualify as legitimate members of the family of God. It emphasizes a truth that is implied in Scripture, but it is not specified as an explicit command in order for a person to receive salvation. There is a verse which states that Jesus will dwell in our hearts through faith, and we assume that He cannot do so unless He is specifically invited (Eph. 3:17). God graciously offers salvation to anyone who has sincerely confessed or called upon the name of the Lord in repentance and believed with their hearts that God raised Him from the dead (Acts 2:21,38; 8:37; Rom. 10:9-10). Heaven will be filled with people who never formally asked Jesus into their hearts but did regularly confess the Apostle's Creed and repeat the confessions of repentance in their prayer books with sincerity of faith from their hearts.

2) Misconception: We do not need to be concerned about

the backslidden because "Once saved, always saved" is a reliable doctrine. After all, in John 10:28-29 Jesus did say that no man could pluck a person from His Father's hands.

Idle reliance on this doctrine carries considerable risks if other scriptures are reliable. It is true that no man could pluck a person's salvation from the hand of God. However, the Bible does say that in the end times some would be deceived and deliberately depart from the faith (1 Tim. 4:1). When the Word speaks about the faith, it means faith in the Lord Jesus as Savior and Lord of one's life. The book of Jude speaks about false teachers that it terms as "twice dead" because they had a doom of everlasting darkness awaiting them (Jude 1:12-13). The phrase "twice dead" could only refer to those who have once been saved and made alive in the spirit by faith in Christ. Before a person is born again, they are dead in their trespasses and sins though they are alive physically (Eph. 2:1). Salvation brings them to life spiritually. If they have arrived at a condition wherein they are again dead but yet are still alive physically, it strongly suggests that they have experienced spiritual death for a second time. In the book of Revelations, Jesus told the people of the church at Sardis that those who overcame sin and repented would not have their names blotted out of the Book of Life (Rev. 3:5-6). Jesus does not make idle threats; He would never say this if it were not a possibility that their names could be removed. Therefore, all sincere believers should ask the Lord to give them a heart to intercede for backsliders.

3) **Misconception: I really am challenged when people in church testify about witnessing to strangers about salvation through Jesus. I feel like a spiritual misfit because I am uncomfortable about initiating spiritual conversations with people whom I do not know.**

The concept that it is everyone's Christian duty to perpetually present the plan of salvation to total strangers brings condemnation to many faithful believers. It is interesting to note that though many testify about such ventures, few are successful in getting their subjects into fellowship as true converts from sin to Christ. Perhaps the reason for this is that we are attempting to provide spiritual answers for people who are not directing spiritual questions to us. Religious issues are intimate matters that most people are uncomfortable about discussing with those whom they do not know. Jesus instructed His apostles that when they went out to evangelize a city, they were to make inquiries about people who were known to be worthy persons. The word "worthy" can be translated "suitable." The implication is that Jesus was instructing His men to identify with people who were suitable in that they were well known for their interest in spiritual things (Matt. 10:11-12; Luke 10:5-7). This is a wise strategy. This type of person normally can introduce one to their circles of friends with similar interests.

Paul followed this tactic on his missionary journeys. He would first go to the local synagogues in the cities where he wished to plant churches (Acts 17:1-3). In Philippi, he initiated the ministry by going to the place where people regularly met for prayer (Acts 16:12-13). He chose the synagogue and the Areopagus in Athens as good places to encounter those who had already demonstrated an interest in eternal matters. There he found notable men who spent their days discussing religion and philosophy (Acts 17:16-21). On other occasions, he stimulated people's interest by performing miracles of healing. When they saw the signs and wonders, they became interested in what Paul had to say (Acts 28:1-10; Rom. 15:18-19). The exception to this strategy may be Philip the evangelist. He went to Samaria and simply began to preach Christ. He was set in the Body of Christ as an evangelist, and those who heard him believed his message because they saw visible demonstrations of the power of God (Acts 8:5-7; 21:8).

All Christians should be able to present the Gospel message to others, but not all are gifted as an evangelist. Those who have this gift are comfortable talking to anyone, any time, and under any circumstance about their need of salvation. These people have the courage, the grace, and the fruit to vindicate their calling. The rest of us need not be under condemnation when we fail to get excited about door to door, cold-call witnessing outreaches. If we are faithful to pray for lost souls and are prepared to show them the way of salvation, the Holy Spirit will either prompt unsaved acquaintances to ask about our faith or give us opportunities to initiate spiritual conversations.

4) **Misconception: Gentile Christians have a responsibility to confront Jews with the Gospel so they can be transformed into completed Jews.**

Many contemporary evangelicals find it difficult to understand the Jew's aversion to the Christian faith and the name of Jesus. They are often mystified as to why their enthusiastic expressions of Jesus' love are met with a cold shoulder and in some instances mocking hostility. I believe that there are several reasons for this. One is that Jews are insulted by the concept that Gentiles could lead them into any experience that could make them any more Jewish than they were by birth. The Apostle Paul certainly had an excellent understanding of the terms "Jews," "Israelites," and "Hebrews." He claimed to be all three. Though he was born of the tribe of Benjamin, he proclaimed before all that he was a Hebrew of Hebrews, an Israelite, and a Jew (Rom. 11:1; Philip. 3:5; Acts 21:39).

Simply stated, the words "Jew" and "Jewish" refer to religion and culture; "Hebrew" and "Hebrews" refer to a language and a genealogy which can be traced back to Abraham and Isaac; and "Israelites" are those born to citizens of Israel or within Israel's borders.

The second reason is the negative imprint that has been made in the name of Christ on the collective Jewish psyche over the past two millennia. Historically, Christians have demonstrated anything but the love of God to the Jews. Under the banner of the Church and our loyalty to Jesus, we have either actively participated in or ignorantly allowed the persecution of the Jews in nearly every nation that calls itself Christian. Our unscriptural, anti-Semitic theology has paved the way for habitual expressions of social degradation, conversions coerced through torture, and unjust exiles. For centuries, misguided Christians chose the holidays of Christmas and Easter as occasions to perpetrate barbarous crimes against the Jews who lived among them. Because of this, one could say that it is as though there is something in most every Jew's historical and spiritual DNA structure which interprets the Cross as a symbol of disaster. When they are confronted with the Gospel, especially through a Gentile, there is something that is alerted within their souls which says, "danger, danger—fight or flee." This phenomenon could be compared to the ability of various species within creation to adapt to their environments. If there is a poisonous plant indigenous to an area, all the animals learn to avoid it over time. Once the adaptation is secure, an alarm imprint within their DNA causes all future generations to have an aversion to that which their ancestors found toxic.

The third reason is due to the prophetic timing of God's plan for a mass ingathering of the Jewish people before the Second Advent of Christ. This is a privilege that the Lord has reserved for Himself. In perfect timing with His prophetic clock, He will bring the Jews into His flock through a global move of the Holy Spirit on Jewish hearts. The Lord will meet them in divine visitations as He did with Jacob and the Apostle Paul. He will begin to take them aside individually to reveal Himself to them as their Messiah. These private encounters will be much like that of Joseph when he made his identity known to his brothers in Egypt. As the Messiah's identity is made known to their spirits, they will look on Him whom they pierced and mourn. Jesus will comfort them by telling them that though they ignorantly meant it for evil, that God meant it for good. In a relatively short time, millions of Jews will pass under the rod and into the bond of the New Covenant (Eze. 20:33-37). They are the natural branches of the olive tree that will be grafted in among us who are the wild olive branches. Their initial rejection of the Gospel brought us salvation. Their acceptance will usher in new dynamics of spiritual vibrancy to the ministries of the Church (Rom. 11:11-12,15,23).

God blesses those who bless the Jewish people (Gen. 12:3). The Scriptures give ample precedents that the Father's blessings of prosperity, physical healing, and household salvation will increase in the lives of those who do so. Psalms 122:6-9 implies that as we love Israel and pray for her, prosperity will be our reward. When the Jewish elders of Jesus' day wanted Him to come and heal a Gentile centurion's servant, they knew that they would have to give Him a good reason. When Jesus heard that the man loved the Jewish people and had built them a synagogue, He sent the spirit of faith for healing to the man's home and healed the servant (Luke 7:2-10). The first occurrence of the Holy Spirit being poured out on Gentiles to bring salvation and the baptism in the Holy Spirit to an entire neighborhood was prompted by the righteous acts of one Gentile man toward the Jewish people. The angel of the Lord clearly told Cornelius that his gifts to the Jews had come before God as a memorial of his kindness. As a result, God graced all of his friends and relatives with the gift of eternal life (Acts 10:1-5,24; 34-48).

.

Chapter 15

The New Age And Other Religions

I am persuaded that there is a field, ripe for harvest, that is being woefully neglected by the Church at large—the New Age movement. In some regards, we have antagonized and alienated them from perceiving us as friendly people who are open to dialogue. I am not suggesting that we need to compromise the tenets of our faith that compel us to believe that Jesus is the only answer for man's need of eternal salvation. I do, however, believe that we would be wise to consider fresh methods in which to approach these who are already seeking spiritual reality. There must be a non-confrontational way to do it, which does not condescendingly disqualify their journeys and all of their experiences. It is an insult to basic human dignity for another person to dismiss one's journey as valueless. This is especially offensive when the "offender" may not be apparently demonstrating any greater quality of life.

I would like to take you through a brief line of reasoning from Scripture. It could possibly serve to help us discover a way to give these people a little breathing room in relation to some of their experiences. John 10:1-10 tells the story of those who climbed into the sheepfold by circumventing the door of the Messiah. It clearly labels them as thieves and robbers. It is noteworthy that though they were thieves who had the potential to lead others into destruction, nonetheless they were successful in their climbing efforts, although their stay within the sheepfold might have been brief. Generations of them repeatedly sought to slip in to steal something that they discerned as valuable. It could be that though their methods were illegitimate, they managed to touch the edges of legitimate spiritual reality while they were in the sheepfold. God is kind even to the evil (Lk. 6:35). In His mercy, He might have allowed some to experience spiritually viable truths that would serve as seeds to put a permanent longing in them for more such experiences. All they needed was someone to show them the way by using biblical methods.

This might be the situation with what some in the New Age movement report. God's goodness allowed them to taste tidbits of the spiritual realities of the Kingdom so that they might later come to faith and repentance (Rom. 2:4). What they need is dialogue with those who understand what they have seen and are able to point them to its fullness through salvation in Christ. It is doubtful that we will be participants in such discussions if we persist in labeling everything they have experienced as demonic.

1) Misconception: All religions are basically similar in that they all worship the same God. Everyone should explore the various religions and choose the one that best suits their personal interest and needs.

This posture can have tragic eternal consequences. Jesus said that the gate that leads to eternal life in heaven is narrow, and the path that leads to eternal destruction is broad (Matt. 7:13-14). The Bible portrays faith in the name of Jesus as the only true path to eternal life (John 14:6; Acts 4:10-12). Jesus clearly stated that anyone who knew God the Father would recognize Him as God's Son (John 8:19; 1 John 5:11-12). The Word of God describes all of the founders of religions that offer alternate routes to heaven as thieves and robbers (John 10:1,7-11). Paul said that those who worshipped idols were actually worshipping demons rather than the true God (1 Cor. 10:20-22).

The pursuit of God is not something that anyone should take casually in attempts to suit their own interests. Jesus said that the false could be discerned from the true by examining their respective fruit (Matt. 7:15-29). A cursory look at the conditions in non-Christian nations can help one distinguish good fruit from bad fruit and prompt them to make a decision for Christ (Psa. 74:20). The value of Hinduism can be seen as people starve while cattle roam India's streets. Apparently, as some of their ancient holy men meditated, mystical voices spoke and instructed them on holiness. "Do not eat the holy cattle. Kiss the cobras and worship the monkeys as they, too, are holy." Practices like voodoo have reduced Haiti and other nations to abject poverty. Islam leads the way in threatening the world with terrorism. The Buddhist and Taoist of the Far East are long on contemplation and short on acts of mercy. Seldom, if ever, does one hear that these religions have organized relief efforts to aid the victims of natural disasters in foreign nations. On the other hand, wherever there is human need, you can likely find those whom Christ has called to minister His mercy.

2) Misconception: The Bible gives hints that there could be validity to belief in reincarnation.

"Reincarnation" can be defined as the passing of a dead person's soul/spirit into another person's body on the occasion of their conception. It is called the "transmigration of the soul" if the spirit of the deceased is passed on to a form of insect or animal life. According to Eastern mysticism, these processes continue until a spirit inhabits a person who lives a perfect life of good deeds. At this juncture, the process ceases because the spirit deserves to become part of the "cosmic consciousness"— God.

This philosophy is a direct assault against the atoning work of Jesus Christ on the cross and what the Bible says about the finality of physical death. Regardless of one's good deeds, it is appointed to all men to die only once (Heb. 9:27). There would be no need for the sacrificial death of Jesus if man could be joined to the family of God by any means other than belief in His deity, sinless life, burial, and resurrection. Faith in Christ declares an end of trusting in any performance system to achieve peace and unity with God (Rom. 10:4). There is no other means of salvation other than faith through confessing His name (Acts 4:12; Rom. 10:9-10).

Matthew 17:10-13 is the passage that is most often cited to support the claim that reincarnation is a biblical concept. It relates an occasion in which the disciples questioned Jesus about the ancient prophecy that Elijah would return before the end of the age. His response was that this had already occurred, and they understood that He was speaking of the ministry of John the Baptist. A number of factors reveal that the Lord was not endorsing the theory that John the Baptist was the reincarnation of Elijah the prophet. Before John's birth, his father had been told that John would minister in the spirit and power of Elijah the prophet (Luke 1:16-17). The phrase "in the spirit and power" does not indicate reincarnation. It refers to a similarity in anointing for ministry. It was a common event in biblical times for people to operate under the same anointing that some predecessor had carried. This happened with Joshua and the 70 elders due to the fact that Moses laid hands upon them (Num. 11:16-17; Deut. 34:9).

In order for a reincarnation to occur, it would necessitate the death of one person so their spirit can be passed on to another. John the Baptist could not have possessed the personal spirit of Elijah because Elijah never actually died. He had been taken into heaven by the Lord's chariot while alive (2 Kings 2:11-12). When Jesus made the statement in reference to Elijah, King Herod had recently executed John. Subsequent to his execution, the apostles saw Elijah and Moses while Jesus was being transfigured (Matt. 17:1-4). If John had the spirit of Elijah in the reincarnation sense, it would have been John rather than Elijah who would have appeared to Jesus with Moses during His transfiguration.

A physical body cannot sustain life without its spirit. Immediately subsequent to the resurrection of Jesus, many of the Old Testament saints arose from their graves and were seen walking the streets of Jerusalem (Matt. 27:52-53). If reincarnation were a viable concept, their personal spirits would have been residing in people who were living at the time of the resurrection. These living people would have dropped dead when the Old Testament saints were resurrected because their spirits would have to vacate their bodies to enter their former hosts. The Bible makes no mention of phenomena of this magnitude occurring. Furthermore, the Second Coming of Christ and its accompanying resurrection and rapture of millions of dead Christians would have been foretold as a catastrophic event. If reincarnation were factual, millions of innocent people would die as their spirits vacated their bodies to take up residence in the resurrected bodies of their former hosts.

3) Superstition: The psychic abilities that some people have are God-given gifts. When these people are born-again and filled with the Spirit, their abilities become sanctified and enhanced by the power of the Holy Spirit.

This doctrinal misconception is built upon a lack of knowledge about the works of the flesh, the nature of our salvation, and the source of the gifts of the Holy Spirit. If a person is converted to Christ, they were appointed before time began to receive a specific calling and spiritual gifts (2 Tim. 1:9). Simultaneous with their conversion and infilling by the Holy Spirit, their calling and election were made sure by adoption into the family of God (Eph. 1:3-6,13). Prior to the moment of their new birth and adoption by the Father, they were called but nonetheless dead in their trespasses and sins (2:1-2,12-13). Any psychic abilities that they possessed were soulish works of the flesh that were likely enhanced by evil spirits of divination (Acts 16:16-19).

All of the works of the flesh are corruptions of legitimate aspects of human nature (Gal. 5:19-21). For instance, outbursts of anger and adultery are works of the flesh that are condemned. At the same time, everyone has a legitimate capacity to feel the emotions of true righteous anger and to express sexual desires through the marriage covenant. In the same way, every person has a basic ability in their souls to anticipate what is about to happen. Most people can relate to isolated incidences where they sensed something was going to be said or happen before it occurred. If these occasional incidences are not sought or encouraged, they are harmless natural functions of the human soul. However, if a person becomes enamored with the novelty of these phenomena and seeks to experience them, it becomes a work of the flesh. If this flirtation is prolonged, they will inevitably attract a demonic spirit of witchcraft. James 3:15 explains the process as a downward spiral. It begins in the earthly or natural realm, then progresses into sensual or soulish works of the flesh, and finally becomes demonically energized.

The true gifts of God are not upgraded versions of pre-salvation abilities; they are called charisma or grace gifts. The

Greek word *charis* means grace. Adding the suffix *ma,* it means that grace has been made evident. When one receives the baptism of the Holy Spirit, they receive a number of charismatic gifts (1 Cor. 12:1-11). The Holy Spirit will not impart these gifts to anyone who has not received the grace for salvation through Christ (John 1:17). Some object to this reasoning on the basis that what they heard from a psychic was true. Psychic gifts may be accurate, but they are illegitimate because they are generated from a demonic source. The Apostle Paul expelled a spirit of divination out of a fortuneteller who called him a servant of the most high God (Acts 16:16-19). Her words were true, but her information came from an evil spirit. If you have consulted a psychic, renounce it as sin. If you have their resource material, destroy it (Acts 19:18-19).

4) **Superstition: My wife and I were in a faith seminar that was supposedly Christian. One of the speakers began to talk about creative visualization as a tool of faith. We immediately left the service because this is a New Age concept that has no foundation in the Bible.**

Unfortunately, many sincere Christians have avoided visualization for fear of entanglement with New Age mentality. The New Age brand of creative visualization is at best limited, as its source is exaggerated confidence in the power of the human mind. Christian visualization is far different. Our faith is not in the creative power of our thoughts, but rather in the faithfulness of the Almighty Creator to respond to our faith visualizations of His Person and Word for our good.

The Psalms are resplendent with examples of David's creative visualizations. In Psalms 91:4, his meditation was that he could find refuge under the feathers of the Lord's wings. But God is not a big bird. We are created in God's image; we do not have feathers and neither does He. In Psalms 52:8, David envisioned himself like a green olive tree flourishing in the house of the Lord. The symbols of the feathered wings and the olive tree, which he painted on the canvas of his imagination, helped David build his faith to flow in the protection and righteousness of God.

Satanic mimicry should never thwart the exploration of legitimate scriptural tools. Moses fearlessly continued in faith when the magicians of Pharaoh duplicated the first three signs that God had commissioned him to perform (Ex. 7-8). They turned rods into serpents, water into blood, and called forth the plague of frogs. Moses did not flee for fear that he had somehow been duped into using occult methods. He continued in faith until God enabled him to do something that the magicians could not duplicate.

Chapter 16

Our Testimony With Those Who Do Not Understand

Even though I am a clergyman by profession, I spend as much time with unbelievers as I do with my fellow saints. Observing these people, I have decided that those who flow in and out of our churches represent approximately 20% of the general population. They have an innate propensity to be interested in spiritual matters. If they were not Christians, they would be involved in some other form of organized religion. The other 80% consists of people who do not have any perceptible interest in spirituality. They are untouched by the spiritual stimuli, which invigorates the other 20%. They do not understand our language, our anger, or our need to incessantly express our spiritual convictions. They shudder at the thought of wasting an hour in a church. The majority of them flip past Christian TV channels quicker than you can say "send in your offering."

One could easily write them off by saying that the natural man does not understand the things of the Lord because they are spiritually discerned (1 Cor. 2:14). However, the Bible also says that God has set eternity in the heart of every person and that deep calls to deep (Eccles. 3:11; Psa. 42:7). The Lord has promised that He would pour out His Spirit upon all flesh. It is reasonable to assume that all flesh includes those who are not spiritually minded naturally. Apparently, when they are immersed with His Spirit, it will satisfy their deep longings for something eternal that they were not even aware that they had. The living waters of salvation through Christ will permanently quench the unidentified thirst in their lives, which they attempted to quench through non-spiritual means.

If we are to hold these people's interest after the Spirit has apprehended them, we are going to have to discover a better way to present true fullness of life. Only a new paradigm of what the Christian life is all about can accomplish this. Most likely what we need is a new reformation within the Church— a reformation into the fullness of life that Jesus promised. Then we will be able to touch the untouched.

1) **Misconception: Christians have a responsibility to confront the abortionist and those seeking abortions with the truth of the Word of God. It clearly states that abortion is murder.**

Unquestionably it is murder to end a human life for the sake of convenience. The global epidemic of abortion is grievously tragic. What many sincere Christians fail to understand is that the unconverted do not regard the Bible as an authoritative directive for their lives. They do not have the capacity to take our quoting of Bible texts any more seriously than we would appreciate a Muslim's quotations of the Islamic Koran. For this reason, it may be more productive if Christians would peacefully approach these people on the basis of moral and ethical values that are supported by the Scriptures rather than actual biblical quotations. There is a spiritual principle that implies that people can often better understand spiritual truths if they are first presented with natural phenomena that punctuate the spiritual realities (1 Cor. 15:46; Eph. 5:31-32). We do have ample data based on secular observations that indicate traumatic consequences to abortion. Early term babies can feel the pain of abortive procedures. Women who have had abortions do tend to have increased instances of depression and reproductive disorders. The courts do award punitive settlements against motorists who recklessly cause the termination of wanted pregnancies. If it is wrong to take an infant's life through a reckless driving accident, why is it not equally immoral to take a life through an intentional medical procedure? If these aforementioned factors are gently presented, they can appeal to the consciences and self-interests of those who give and seek abortions. Once they recognize that the advisor is sensible and has a genuine interest in them, their hearts may be open to hear about the love of God and salvation through faith in Christ.

The Bible does not specifically address abortion, though it was a common practice in ancient times. Their methods were cruelly inhumane. An unwanted child that did not succumb to primitive abortion procedures would be abandoned in a desolate area to perish by the elements and beasts. Nonetheless, there are no New Testament references to indicate that Christians publicly protested against these practices. Under the Old Covenant, abortion was not an issue since the punishment for pre-marital promiscuity and marital infidelity was stoning (Deut. 22:20-22).

2) **Misconception: Christians should use their influence to bar homosexuals from vocations where they could contaminate our children. In addition, they are at high risk for catastrophic illnesses due to their abominable lifestyles. It is unfair for them to be included in our health benefit plans as they raise the rates for everyone else.**

The open hostility between the Church and the homosexual community is a travesty for which conservative Christians are primarily responsible. It is a travesty that we have conditioned a significant portion of the population, which needs Jesus, to interpret His Church as a bastion of condemnation rather than grace. It appears that we have forgotten a number of things. People who have not been born again do not have the capacity to understand righteous behavior from our perspective (1 Cor. 2:14). Those of us who have become new creations in Christ cannot expect others to have the same desires to live righteously that we do. Homosexuality is a form of fornication, which is the general term used in the Bible to denote all unlawful sex acts. Paul exhorted the Ephesians that it was a forbidden practice among Christians (Eph. 5:3-8; 1 Cor. 6:9-11). He gave no hint that we should be scandalized by its presence among unbelievers. The New Testament has many examples of apostolic admonishments for Christians to flee from specific sins. There are no examples of the apostles confronting the unconverted with the wickedness of a specific sin. Apparently the early church leaders understood that if visitors were insulted and condemned throughout a sermon, they would be unlikely to respond positively to the invitation at the end of the sermon.

A reputation for being merciful will always triumph over a reputation for austere judgment. God is kind toward the evil in that He demonstrates His mercy toward them which, in turn, leads them to repentance (Luke 6:35; Ja. 2:13; Rom. 2:4). It is improbable that the Church can convince homosexuals that we love them if we constantly attempt to limit their employment and rights to health care. Their cynicism is justified when we claim that we serve a loving God who supplies all of our needs and then begrudge them for being responsible for raising our insurance rates by a miniscule percentage (Philip. 4:19; 2 Cor. 9:8).

It might be good to keep in mind that the same portion of the book of Romans that traces the roots of unrighteousness mentions being unloving and unmerciful as equally sinful as homosexuality (Rom. 1:18-2:3). In fact, this portion of Scripture says that we have no right to judge others for practicing sins in which we ourselves engage (Rom. 2:1-3). It is a sad commentary, but professing Christians are frequently found guilty of covertly practicing every form of fornication including homosexuality. It is not unusual for it to be discovered that a religious leader ministered effectively for years before his duplicity was uncovered. The adults that sat under his ministry and the children who were raised under him seldom had a clue about the hidden sin. They were blessed by the ministry of these individuals and assumed that they were just as they represented themselves to be.

The Church has an obligation to endeavor to see that no person who practices any form of sexual immorality be hired by institutions that are defined as Christian. But we are not at liberty to put the same standard on non-Christian businesses and institutions. The employees of any type of organization have the right to expect that anyone who is discovered trying to sexually seduce others will be disciplined. The statistics indicate that heterosexuals are much more prone to attempt to seduce the innocent than homosexuals are. Homosexuality is a grievous sin, and those who do not repent of it will spend eternity in hell. Their place in eternal torment will be no more or no less intense than that of heterosexuals who rejected Christ (Rev. 21:8; 22:14-15).

3) Misconception: The liberals need to understand that the answer to our nation's ills is a Christian government.

This will be true during the millennial reign of Jesus Christ. The theological term for a religious system being the primary influence in a nation's government is "sacralism." Within sacral governments, the Church plays the primary role in appointing civil authorities, and they reciprocate by enforcing the Church's doctrines and policies. Nations ruled by Islamic fundamentalists are contemporary examples of this system. The Roman Empire, ancient Germany, Switzerland, and Britain were sacral governments. Historically, this form of administration has not proven to be friendly for Christians who were progressive in their faith. The Romans threw them to the lions. It was the sacralists of England who drove the Pilgrims to America's shores. Candidly speaking, there is a sinister force of pride that seems to emerge from the corporate mentalities of religious groups and their leaders when they taste political power and begin to sense that they are flowing in the approval of God and man. The Protestant reformers, Calvin of Switzerland and Luther of Germany, were both born-again men with notable spiritual insights. Nonetheless, they orchestrated the civil arrest and torture of fellow Christians who differed with them doctrinally. With this enigma in mind, it is not inconceivable to consider the possibility that some of our spiritual leaders might respond to political power in a similar fashion.

For instance, some of the major leaders of the religious right are doctrinally fundamentalists. It is not unusual for them to preach that Pentecostal and Charismatic believers are suffering from emotional, and, in some cases, demonic illusions. Conversely, Christians of Pentecostal and Charismatic persuasions often label the fundamentalists as neo-Pharisees. The classic differences between these groups have split hundreds of churches and marred countless lifelong friendships with bitter suspicions. If either group were to achieve major political power, it would not be unrealistic for the other group, along with members of anti-religious organizations, to become apprehensive about being targeted for persecution as members of subversive factions.

It is interesting to note that though Israel under the Old Covenant had a sacral government, the early Church of the New Covenant did not attempt to continue it. To the contrary, Jesus proclaimed that if His Kingdom were of this world, His disciples would fight (John 18:36). The apostles did preach that Jesus was the ruler of all the kings of the earth, but there is no evidence that they encouraged their followers to push for major political power as His delegates. Paul taught that all governmental authorities were appointed servants of God who should be honored (Rom. 13). It was the Roman government that he was endorsing as divinely appointed.

The democratic governments that many Christians decry in public protest today pale in comparison to the corruption, occult contamination, unjust excessive taxation, and sexual perversion of the Roman Empire. Perhaps everyone would rest easier if the Church blessed its nation's politicians and ruled through prayer rather than overt political power (1 Tim. 2:1-4; Eph. 1:18-23; 2:4-7).

Chapter 17

Business Life

One of the most common areas where Christians come into conflict one with another is the business arena. Through the years I have served as an arbitrator to settle disputes between believers in various corporations and business ventures which represented over $20,000,000 worth of investment capital. It has been rewarding to see some situations turn from potential disaster to tranquil prosperity. Unfortunately, in all too many instances, it has been frustrating and heartrending to see friendships and dreams shattered, homes go through foreclosure, and life savings lost. In these cases, individual's naive understandings of how to bring spiritual dynamics to the marketplace tended to intensify complex issues rather than defuse them.

It is my observation that there are two major areas where Christians are prone to have naive misconceptions about business. One is that they often underestimate the generous measure of wisdom with which God has anointed the secular market. The Scripture confirms that the unrighteous are generally wiser about making and handling money than the righteous (Luke 16:8; Prov. 20:14). Carnal greed is not normally the motivating factor when secular businesses determine their profit margins. When items carry a 40%–60% mark-up over their purchase price, it is because that is what is needed to cover legitimate overhead. These seemingly high percentages enable firms to cover the losses of merchandise that does not sell and capital to buy more merchandise, pay salaries, rent, social security contributions, and provide profits for the owners and investors. Ironically, Christian merchants who intend to demonstrate love for people and disdain for the world by slashing prices often unwittingly doom their businesses. Secondly, some believers mistakenly presume that salvation exempts them and those they hire, from the need of hands-on experience in a particular market. One's faith in Christ does not override the value of disciplined faithfulness to learn under the tutelage of those who are accomplished (Luke 16:12). Many businesses fail because they prefer spirituality over expertise in those they hire.

Here is a brief illustration. There was a Christian inventor who began to manufacture his brilliantly designed institutional-sized trash compactor. It was his dream to bless other believers, so he franchised it exclusively among Christians. His prices did not realistically compensate for his overhead. Several men from a church in a major city bought a franchise and an inventory of compactors. None of them had ever been in that field or had investigated the market in their city. They enthusiastically attempted to present their product to hotels, hospitals, and civil institutions. The doors that they had anticipated would swing open to them never even cracked open sufficiently to give them serious consideration. Finally they did get several contracts that were abruptly canceled with vague explanations. Several days later two well-dressed men who said they were "union officials" visited them. They explained that the institutional market was under long-term contract to a "family-owned" trash removal company. The callers conveyed that it would be best for all concerned for them to seek another line of business. That was 20 years ago. As far as I know, their inventory of trash compactors is still rusting in the lot of one of the investors. The manufacturer has long since declared bankruptcy. Of course, the whole matter was attributed to the devil working through the city's criminal element. I believe that he was also working through their naivete and lack of market knowledge prior to making an investment.

1) Misconception: Believers should always favor Christian merchants, professionals, and tradesmen with their business.

Ideally speaking, this is true (Gal. 6:10). The problem is that we are living in an age wherein many Christian business people have yet to grasp the idea of doing their work with excellence as unto the Lord (Col. 3:23). Many believers have met with disappointment and frustration in their attempts to deal exclusively with Christians. Frequently they find that fellow believers are as apt as unbelievers to produce shoddy workmanship and are less than candid about their ability to meet delivery schedules. When they are called into account, some tend to offer a host of spiritual excuses as well as the routine worldly ones. "The devil has been hindering our work schedule, and we need prayer." "I was witnessing to an unsaved mechanic while doing your oil change and inadvertently forgot to put in the oil filter. Please forgive me. I'll be happy to give you 20% off on a new engine."

A good rule of thumb is to inquire about the track record of those with whom you anticipate doing business. If they appear to be using Christianity as an advertisement to generate business, double-check their references. Perhaps the wisest policy is to seek out those who have reputations for excellence in their field. If you later discover that they happen to be professing Christians, it will be an added blessing.

2) Misconception: The market value of my car is $5,000, and I really need to get at least that for it. Deacon Jones is in dire need of a car, but he has only got $2,000. I think I should sell it to him.

It is more blessed to give than receive. Charitable giving is a virtue that all Christians need to cultivate (Acts 20:35; 2 Cor. 9:6). Spontaneous offerings can be a source of blessing for both the giver and the recipient (Matt. 6:3; 2 Cor. 9:8). The primary mode, however, that the Scriptures encourage is giving with predetermined purpose much like a farmer sows seed. This being true, the best time to determine what one will give is prior to an event rather than in the middle of it (2 Cor. 9:5,7). Good stewardship over one's resources is no less a spiritual value than giving (1 Cor. 4:2, Prov. 27:23-24). If you need to get a certain price for an item in order to keep your budget in line when replacing it, wise stewardship dictates that you hold out in faith for your asking price. A good motto is: "Keep business as business and charity as charity." One of the reasons for this can be seen in the scenario of selling the car to Deacon Jones. It is not uncommon for there to be unforeseen repercussions in selling a used car. If the car breaks down, the buyer can easily expect the seller to make it right without regard to the grace motivated reduced price which they originally paid. It could be that the owner of the car and Deacon Jones would be best served if the car were sold for $5,000 to another person. The seller could then give the deacon an offering from it. He would be blessed for his charity, and the grateful recipient would be able to buy a better car than he might have otherwise been able to afford.

3) Misconception: Declaring bankruptcy is an untenable option for Christians. It demonstrates a blatant lack of faith in God's ability to supply all of our needs.

God's faithfulness to supply all of our needs is an absolute, but most would agree that there are instances where His timing in doing so can be an uncomfortable variable. Bankruptcy should never be pursued as an easy way out of one's obligations, but it is a biblical concept. This is demonstrated through the law of Jubilee, which God gave to His covenant people Israel. Every 50th year, all that anyone had lost was restored regardless of whether they had lost it through ineptness or adverse business conditions. The providential love of God anticipated people's capacity to succumb to the pressures of life so He devised a means of escape for them. Those who were mired in debt could deed their property, or family members as indentured servants to their creditors. In the year of Jubilee, the creditors were obligated by law to restore their houses, lands, and children to them without further recourse (Lev. 25:28,54). In the meantime, those who were poverty stricken had a way of providing for their families. Those who were diligent could make profits in order to become reestablished. For instance, they could glean behind those who were harvesting fields. The harvesters were not allowed to go through the fields a second time because the remaining produce was specifically for the poor (Deut. 24:21). Those who worked hard at gleaning were able to feed themselves and make a living by selling the surplus.

The precarious nature of the marketplace has not changed since biblical times. Eighty percent of business ventures fail within two years. Fifty percent of those that remain do not survive for more than five years. It is not unusual for these factors to be detrimental to the finances of Christians who are employed by these firms. Contemporary Christians have a better covenant than Israel did, and it is established on better promises (Heb. 8:6). It is inconceivable that God would provide a way of escape for the Old Testament saints and subsequently leave

New Covenant believers without recourse. Those in both groups need the hope that if devastating adversity strikes, they will have the option to declare loss and the opportunity to become reestablished without pressure from creditors. Conscientious believers can always choose to repay their former debts when they begin to earn adequate incomes (Rom. 13:8).

4) **Misconception: I hired a Christian, and there was a non-competitive clause in his contract. He recently left my firm to establish the same type of business. He is now calling my clients to secure their accounts. The law is in my favor but I cannot take him to court because the Bible forbids it.**

This is a misconception that has given license for unprincipled people to perpetuate unrestrained mayhem in the lives of professing Christians. The New Testament admonishes those with complaints to first attempt to settle their conflicts through Christian mediation (1 Cor. 6:1-7). This policy was encouraged to spare the redeemed community the embarrassment of having its weaknesses exposed to the world. Those who persisted in their offenses were to be treated as heathens (Matt. 5:25; 18:15-17). This permitted offended persons the option of pursuing the matter in civil court in order to recover legitimate losses.

The concept of lawsuits to recover losses is founded on biblical precedents. The civil judges of ancient Israel were the respected elders of each community. The Law provided that those who lost anything through the negligence of others could turn to the judges to recover the equivalent of their losses (Ex. 21:32-34, 22:1-9).

Chapter 18

Angels And the Hereafter

There are occasions when I inwardly cringe as I hear the remarks that Christians make about heaven. One of these is, "When we get to heaven, we will be able to praise the Lord for all eternity." I know that the remark is an innocent, well-intentioned attempt to express love for God. In part, I identify with it as I delight in the idea that we will have periods of praise in heaven that will eclipse anything we have touched here on earth. At heart, I am a worshipper; I often do it as much out of church as I do in church. Eternity, however, could be described as time in endless duration. Therefore, it is a long time to be occupied with nothing more than praise. My contemplation of their remark makes my spirit reel with thoughts that, if true, heaven might tend to be uncreative and boring. In addition, it is my understanding that the job has been filled for ages as there are seraphim who continuously fly around the throne of God shouting forth utterances of worship (Isa. 6:1-3).

One of the redemptive names of the Lord is Jehovah Elohim. It means the Lord our eternal Creator. The Lord's Prayer instructs us to pray that His will be done on earth as it is in heaven. His name being Eternal Creator denotes that His will in heaven is eternal creativity. Since we are made in His image to please Him forever, I suspect that in heaven we will please Him through creative pursuits just as we do on earth. It is my conviction that our references to heaven would be much more appealing to the unconverted if they contain inklings of exciting eternal occupations.

1) Superstition: Children who die in infancy become little cherubs with angelic wings. Kind people are assigned to serve God as angels in the hereafter.

Mankind and angels are beings of separate, distinct species. Angels were created in heaven in an age before the world was formed. They have celestial bodies that are superior in strength to humans (1 Cor. 15:10; 2 Pet. 2:11). The only angels that have wings are the cherubim and seraphim. The cherubs will have two or four and seraphim have six (1 Kings 6:27; Ezek. 1:6; 10:14; Isa. 6:1-3). Angels, cherubim, and seraphim are all majestic in appearance and sometimes frightening. When angels appeared to biblical characters, it was not uncommon for them to encourage them not to be fearful (Luke 1:13,30).

Humans are created on earth by the natural birth process. If a person of any age dies, their body will remain in the grave until the resurrection of the dead at the end of this age. At death, only their spirits depart into the eternal regions. The spirit of a person has a shape that bears the likeness of their earthly physical form (Luke 16:22-23). Their spirits will remain unattached to a physical body until they are rejoined with their earthly bodies in glorified form in one of the resurrections at the end of this age (1 Thes. 4:13-18; Rev. 20:12-13).

2) Superstition: Those who die violently and those who had unsettled emotions at the time of death turn into ghosts.

Their restless spirits will haunt geographical locations until peace is made on their behalf.

The entities that haunt places are demons that are mimicking the people that they once inhabited. When their hosts died, they lost their dwelling places. Satan uses them to deceive gullible people about the nature and finality of physical death (Eccles. 5:15; Heb. 9:27). The Bible clearly states that death ends a person's ability to directly influence the living (Eccles. 9:5-6,10). It strictly forbids all attempts to communicate with the dead on behalf of the living (Deut. 18:9-14; Isa. 8:19). Any property that is experiencing poltergeist phenomena should be exorcised in the name of Jesus.

3) Misconception: There is no biblical evidence for the phenomena called "near death experiences."

There is a portion of Scripture that mentions the existence of a silver cord that is broken at death when the human spirit returns to God (Eccles. 12:5-7). This cord fits the description of the tunnel of light that people allegedly travel during near death experiences. It might be a type of spiritual umbilical cord that sustains our lives from above while we are living here on earth and provides even the unconverted with the potential for communication from the eternal realm (Job 32:8; 33:4; 34:14). At death, this cord is severed, and the spirit travels up to the eternal realm. When the spirit reaches this realm, it is given directives to go to an abode of bliss or torment. It is possible that God, in His mercy, might give some individuals an event in which their spirits make a partial journey up this cord before it is severed at death. Normally those who have gone through the near death phenomena report that they subsequently viewed their lives and eternity more soberly.

Chapter 19

Foundations for Freedom

Charismatic superstitions and doctrinal misconceptions are commonly spawned as sincere Christians attempt to move in the arena of spiritual revelations in their efforts to help others. This is a biblically legitimate desire that carries the potential risk for both good and deceptive revelations (Heb. 5:12-14). There are three things that are vital for protection against deception. First, humility is a great asset that enables us to listen to our critics with the understanding that God may be subtly using them to caution us. Next, we must never perpetuate doctrines or ministry techniques upon experiences that do not have clear precedents in the Word of God. Third, we must become securely grounded in the foundation doctrines of the Christian faith.

Maturing in the Christian life is similar to adding an addition to your home—both require that you secure a building permit. Cities issue permits to ensure that those who build do so according to code. God requires no less because He loves us too much to chance our moving in the realities of mature revelation if we have faulty foundations. His hesitation is spawned out of His desire to diminish the potential for us to go into fanatical error. Therefore, He will not permit us to receive the insights of the mature unless we are building according to the code of the six foundation doctrines of the Christian faith which are listed in Hebrews 6:1-3. The following is a cursory outline of these basic truths:

I) **Repentance from dead works:** Repentance means to change your mind and direction 180 degrees. God has never changed His mind about man's need to repent as he turns to Christ. In Acts 2:37-39, the religious Jews asked Peter what they must do to receive Christ. The initial word of his response was "repent." The context reveals that it is essential that those whom the Lord calls must repent as they turn to Him. We are to turn from two forms of "dead works." The first type of dead works is any sinful act which we committed when flowing with the spirit of disobedience as it manipulated the desires of our flesh and minds prior to our knowledge of Christ (Eph. 2:1-3). The second type is our attempt to prove ourselves worthy of God's kingdom by any religious act other than faith in Jesus' atoning work of grace on the cross.

2) **Faith toward God:** Our faith is in the lordship of Jesus as the only begotten Son of God and in God as our loving heavenly Father. Our faith is walked out by our ongoing confidence in the reliability of the Scriptures as God's Word and obedience to the Lord's voice.

3) **The doctrine of baptisms:** There are two Baptisms. In each, we are immersed into one of two distinct substances—water or the Holy Spirit.

According to Romans 6:3-4, baptism in water is our identification with the death, burial, and resurrection of the Lord. It is an outward sign of our inward decision to be separated from our old lifestyle and to live in obedience to the Lord.

The baptism in the Holy Spirit is an event subsequent to one's salvation wherein we are filled with the Holy Spirit and empowered with spiritual gifts to assist us in our Christian lives. This experience is not one and the same as receiving the Holy Spirit in the new birth. In Acts 8, the people who had been evangelized and baptized in water under the preaching of Philip later received the infilling of the Spirit through the ministry of Peter and John.

In water baptism, a servant of the Lord immerses us in water. With the baptism of the Holy Spirit, Jesus baptizes us in the Spirit to enable us to demonstrate power as His servants (John 1:33).

4) **Laying on of hands:** We lay hands on people to impart the Holy Spirit and physical healing (Mark 16:17-18; Acts 19:6). The blessing for fruitful lives can be passed from one generation to the next through this sacrament (Gen. 48:8-20). Through the laying on of hands, both spiritual gifts and authority are transmitted from one believer to another (1 Tim. 4:14).

5) **Resurrection of the dead:** There are two distinct resurrections. The first resurrection has three phases: The initial phase took place in a nearly simultaneous manner with Christ's resurrection from the dead when the Old Testament saints who had been waiting in Abraham's bosom/paradise came out of their graves (Matt. 27:52-53). The second phase will occur at what is commonly called "the Rapture" when the bodies of Christians, who have died in the faith subsequent to the ascension of Jesus, will be raised in a glorified, incorruptible form. In heaven, their glorified bodies will be reunited with their spirits and souls that have been with the Lord since their deaths (1 Thes. 4:16-17; 1 Cor. 15:42-44; 2 Cor. 5:8). The third phase

will take place prior to the 1000 year reign of Christ. In it, all believers who perished during the Tribulation will be resurrected (Rev. 20:4-6).

The second resurrection happens after the millennium. This is when all those who have not been resurrected previously will come back to life (Rev. 20:11-15).

6) **The eternal judgment:** There are three judgment seats at which different categories of people will be judged to determine their various rewards or eternal destinies. At the judgment seat of Christ, believers will be judged to determine their rewards in the hereafter (2 Cor. 5:10). At the throne of Christ's glory, nations and their inhabitants will be assessed as to how they treated the Lord's brothers—the Jews and the Christians. Faithful nations will be part of the millennial kingdom (Matt. 25:31-46). The final judgment takes place after the millennium at the great white throne. All those who did not know the Lord will be judged to determine their eternal destiny (Rev. 20:11-15).

The Holy Spirit is poised to grace us with prophetic insights, which we have not known heretofore, that will motivate us with visions for His glory. Let us all pick up the challenge to become fully established in the doctrines which will protect us as we move from glory to glory in revelation.

Christians around the world are being refreshed with a new zeal to lay aside every weight that would hinder them. We would be wise to reevaluate the spiritual authenticity of the beliefs and practices that we have acquired in our Spirit-filled journey. If it becomes apparent that we are needlessly encumbered by some doctrinal misconception or superstition, we should repent of it and renounce it. Then we should make a strong corrective confession of faith based on the principles of

God's Word that reveal the truth. If we know that we have influenced others with an unsound doctrine, it is advisable for us to offer them an update on our position relating to it.

We need not fear deception if we are grounded in the foundations of the faith and continuously cultivate a love for the unadulterated truths of God's Word. Doctrinal misconceptions and superstitions cannot survive the filtering process of the inner witness of the Spirit of truth that is coupled with objective knowledge of the inspired Word of the Lord.

ABOUT THE AUTHOR...

JIM CROFT is also the author of *Heaven on the Links* and *Faith's Decision for the Abundant Life*. His works have been published in eight languages, and he has ministered in scores of nations. He is known worldwide for his unique ability to share profound biblical truths in a simple, interesting and humorous way that encourages people to incorporate them into their everyday lives. Jim and his wife Prudence have been married for over 35 years and have four married daughters, all of whom love the Lord.

SPEAKING ENGAGEMENTS

Jim Croft is available for speaking engagements at churches and conferences. Please send inquiries to:
JCroft8942@aol.com or call 561-852-2155.

OTHER BOOKS BY JIM CROFT

FAITH'S DECISION FOR THE ABUNDANT LIFE
The Lord desires to bless our lives in every way imaginable: emotional well-being, financial prosperity, spiritual blessing, and physical health. It's time to embrace the "whole package"!
ISBN 1-58169-016-9 64 pg. $5.95

HEAVEN ON THE LINKS
A devotional for the avid or beginning golfer. Includes golf tips and thoughtful devotions that speak to the heart of men facing the challenges of today's world.
ISBN #1-58169-015-0 160 pg. $8.95

To purchase these books, visit your local bookstore,
order online at Amazon.com, BN.com, or Borders.com
or call Streamwood Distribution at 888-670-7463.